G000090267

JOURNEY TO KATMANDU

Michael H. C. Baker

DAVID & CHARLES
NEWTON ABBOT LONDON
NORTH POMFRET (VT) VANCOUVER

ISBN 0 7153 6367 0

To my father, who did something similar
fifty years before

Set in 11 on 13pt Imprint and printed in Great Britain by Latimer Trend & Company Ltd for David & Charles (Holdings) Limited South Devon House Newton Abbot Devon

Published in the United States of America by David & Charles Inc North Pomfret Vermont 05053 USA

Published in Canada by Douglas David & Charles Limited 3645 McKechnie Drive West Vancouver BC

Contents

Illustrations

PLATES

IN TEXT

Introduction

In ancient times the road to Kabul and Katmandu was traversed by conquering armies, by refugees, by merchants, by adventurers, by explorers, by men of religion, and by the ordinary citizen going about his everyday business. All these travellers can still be found, even the conquering armies, but this is the story of forty-six young people who followed what has come to be called the 'hippie trail'; although hippies form only a tiny percentage of the many who take the overland route to Nepal.

The reasons why people make this journey vary considerably. For those on their way to Australia, New Zealand or the Far East it may be a cheaper and perhaps more adventurous alternative to flying or going by sea; for some it is a holiday, and for writers, photographers and dealers in various goods it is a means of making a living. For a few—the 'professional' travellers—it is a way of life. They may be hippies—although there are far fewer genuine ones than is generally supposed—they may be the sons or daughters of wealthy and indulgent parents, or they may be people who are for ever on the move, working for a while in one place, moving on, coming to rest to earn money for the next stage, then off again.

There are two principal methods of discovering when such an overland journey is about to begin. The first is from the personal columns of the Sunday papers; the second is via the grapevine which carries news of such ventures. Access to the grapevine is made through people who have already undertaken overland journeys, consequently this method is more likely to provide one with first-hand information as to the chances of a successful outcome of an expedition, whether the costs quoted are reliable, the assurances that there will be no trouble in passing frontiers over-optimistic, and the pedigree of the vehicles in which one is to travel unimpeachable. Nearly all the organisations which advertise in the Sunday papers are perfectly reliable and invite prospective customers to get together and meet the expedition leaders some weeks before the journey starts and before any money has changed hands.

All sorts of vehicles attempt the overland trail, from motor cycles and even bicycles to buses and heavy lorries. At one end of the scale are the one- or two-line advertisements asking for a fourth member to complete a party setting out in a small saloon car, whilst at the other are those which regularly appear promising strict adherence to a firm schedule and offering accommodation in specially built, air-conditioned luxury coaches with many of the overnight stops being at the best class of hotel. The cost can vary from under £50 all in to around £500.

Our expedition got together in a somewhat unexpected setting—a ladies dress shop in Gillingham, Kent, which happened to be the property of the two organisers, Janet and Roger. Janet was a one-time children's nurse who, some years earlier, had gone out from England to Australia and had almost immediately decided she wanted to come home. She could not afford the passage, but had sufficient money to buy a second-hand Land Rover; by taking along three fare-paying passengers, she was able to ship it to India and drive home from there. She had so enjoyed the experience that she had been plying the route ever since in a variety of vehicles, chiefly mini-buses and coaches, sometimes selling the vehicle in Afghanistan or Nepal, sometimes bringing back passengers in it.

Janet was in her late twenties, as was Roger, her partner. He had first made the journey as a fare-paying passenger, and had taken over the driving when the original driver had suddenly handed in his notice in one of the more remote areas of Central Asia. Roger had decided that this was more in his line, at least for the time being, than the textile industry in which he had formerly been employed.

The dress shop in Gillingham had been bought by Janet and Roger out of the proceeds of their earlier expeditions. It was run by Janet's mother when they were out of the country.

Third in command of the expeditions was Jim, who until a year earlier had been an aircraft engineer or, as he put it 'a wind tunnel engineer's mate'. He had joined the organisation in a similar manner to Roger, starting out as a passenger and continuing as a driver. I was the third of the drivers, having given up a post in an art college to see something of the world.

We were proposing to make the journey to Kabul in Afghanistan in three ex-RAF four-wheel-drive lorries. Their accommodation was spartan, consisting merely of wooden benches. The passengers had to be prepared for this and were expected to bring sleeping-bags, blankets and plenty of heavy clothing, which should ensure that they travelled warmly, if not comfortably. Virtually the only modification made to each lorry since its service days was the repainting of its cab. Jim's was white and called Hope, Roger's was blue and named Charity, and mine was red and known as Faith. The lorries were very sound mechanically, and their four-wheel drive and high clearance made them ideal for such a journey.

We calculated it would take around twenty-eight days to reach Kabul and the cost to each passenger would be £25. For this he, or she, would get the barest essentials, that is, travel, visas and a roof—the lorry's canvas canopy—over his head at night.

Nearly everyone who appeared at the preliminary meeting—held on a Sunday four weeks before we were due to leave—was there as a result of our newspaper advertisement, but one or two came because we were known to them through friends who had made previous journeys with Janet and Roger. Inevitably the question most people wanted to ask concerned the dangers which might attend our expedition. One answer was that each year a great many people travelled the route quite safely and that we ourselves had all been before and had returned unscathed.

This was true, but it would be foolish to deny that an overland journey through the heart of Asia could ever be entirely free of

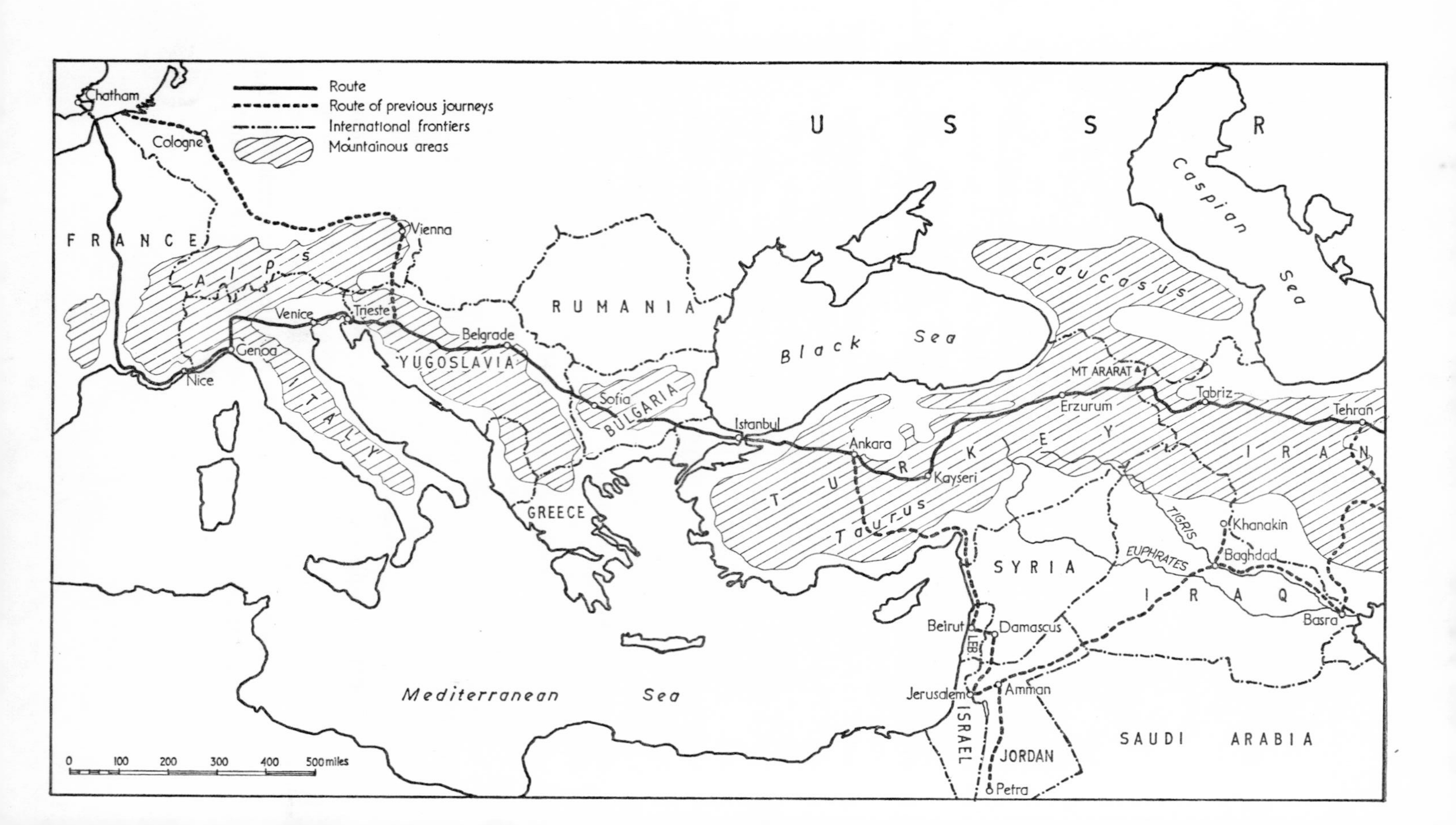
Route
Route of previous journeys
International frontiers
Mountainous areas
U S S R
Caspian Sea
Caucasus
Black Sea
FRANCE
Alps
RUMANIA
YUGOSLAVIA
BULGARIA
ITALY
GREECE
TURKEY
Taurus
IRAN
IRAQ
SYRIA
LEB.
ISRAEL
JORDAN
SAUDI ARABIA
Mediterranean Sea
MT ARARAT
TIGRIS
EUPHRATES
Chatham
Cologne
Vienna
Venice
Trieste
Genoa
Nice
Belgrade
Sofia
Istanbul
Ankara
Kayseri
Erzurum
Tabriz
Tehran
Khanakin
Baghdad
Basra
Beirut
Damascus
Jerusalem
Amman
Petra
0 100 200 300 400 500 miles

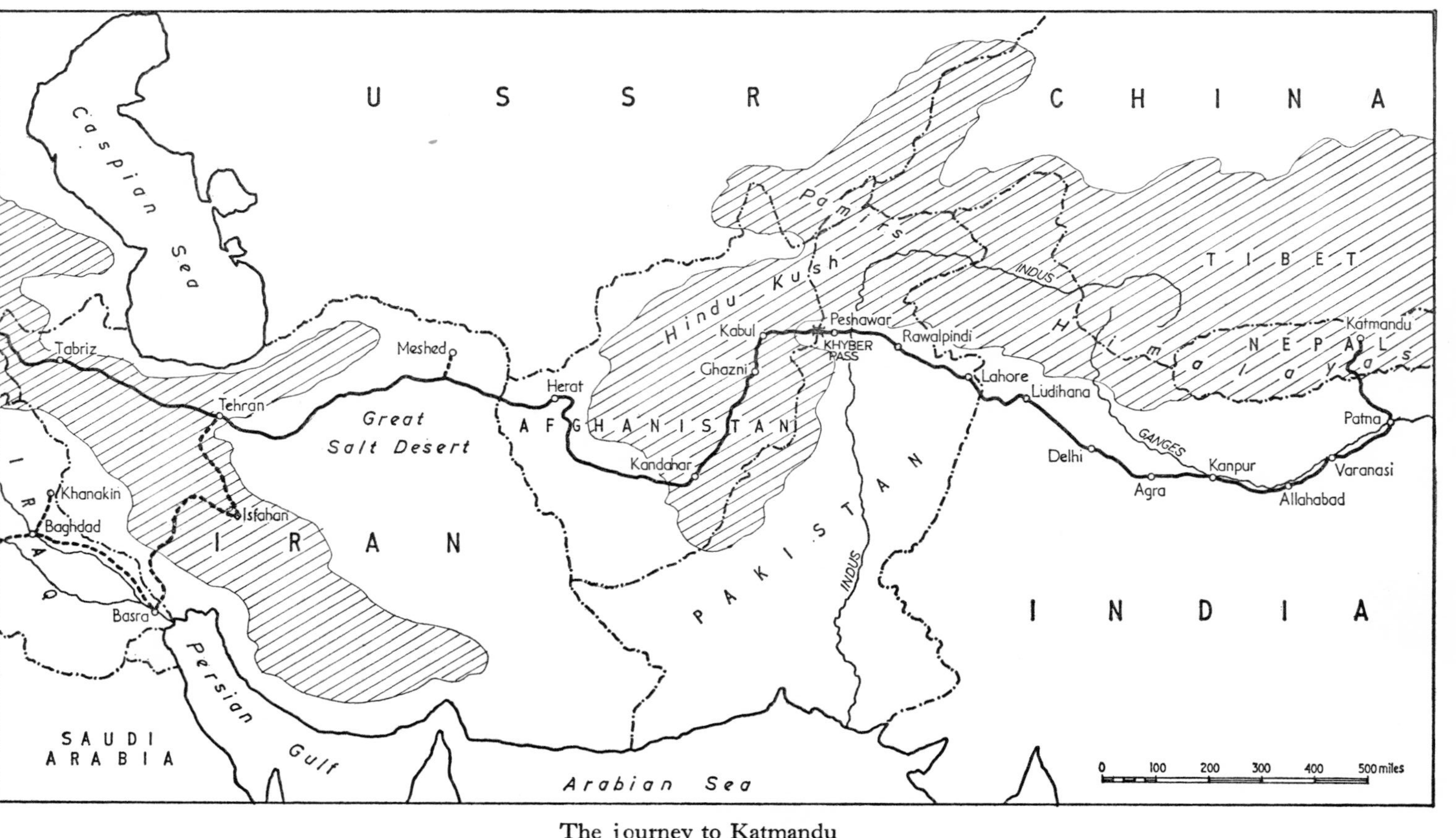

The journey to Katmandu

hazard. Because we would not this time be passing through any of the Arab countries, there was no chance of being chased back to our hotel in Baghdad by a barefoot character toting a rifle, nor was there a risk of being stoned by a band of infuriated tribesmen in Jordan—two incidents from previous expeditions. The Jordanian incident had involved a small boy who stepped out from behind a sandhill in the middle of the desert into the path of Janet's coach; he had been run over and killed. The coach had stopped; members of the boy's tribe had appeared and began to hurl stones through the windows, and there is no knowing what might have happened had not a lorry come upon the scene. The lorry driver told Janet's driver to pull himself together and get away as fast as he could. In Amman the party reported the incident. Janet's driver was arrested and languished in prison for two weeks whilst Janet and the others waited anxiously in a hotel. Eventually his innocence was established and the entire party was invited by King Hussein to a reception at the royal palace.

In Iraq, where all sorts of nasty things can overtake anyone from the head of state to the most innocent bystander, it had been our misfortune on one occasion to get embroiled in the Kurdish problem. The Kurds, who live in eastern Turkey, northern Iraq, and western Iran, have long been pressing for greater autonomy, if not complete independence. The previous October when we arrived on the Iraqi side of the Iranian border, we had been told that we couldn't cross immediately on account of an outbreak of cholera in Baghdad; we later discovered that this had been used as an excuse for indulging in yet one more row between Iraq and Iran over the Kurds.

So we holed up in the frontier post, a mud fort in the middle of a rock-strewn desert, and spent a week staring at the Persian hills a mile off. During this time we had ample opportunity to explore our surroundings. We were at a loss to account for the many pock marks in the wall of our temporary home, until the man in charge of the power station—a bicycle fixed on a stand and pedalled at frequent intervals to drive a dynamo which generated the electricity—told us they were caused by bullets fired by a bunch of Kurds during a raid the previous week. We were given to understand that this was a regular thing and might well be repeated any day. Monotonous though life was at the fort, it was preferable to the perhaps excessive excitement of a siege and, with no sign of the border being opened, we retreated down to the far south of Iraq, crossing into Iran beside the Persian Gulf, far away from the land of the Kurds.

The most likely impediments to an overland journey fall into three categories. The first is the political, as already instanced; the second is the act of God, or more likely the Devil, exemplified by the torrential and quite unheralded storm which, in the middle of the night, washes away one's tent with oneself still in it; and the third is the mechanical, which encompasses anything from a brake failure half-way down the Himalayas to a sudden loss of power when racing a train to a level crossing in India. In actual fact this last hazard is not particularly serious as every crossing-keeper's hut displays a notice informing one that a complaints book is kept within.

Only the wildest optimist would set out in the expectation of dodging every one of such calamities; they are best regarded as character-forming experiences, useful as yardsticks against which to contrast the more serene moments of the journey. If one gets as far as Afghanistan—and not all of Janet's expeditions did—then although one is safe from confrontations with railway trains—there aren't any—one will not necessarily escape acts of God or politicians, or perhaps combinations of the two. The most extreme tend to happen to travellers on their own or in very small groups. They set up camp somewhere out in the wilds and are simply not seen again. That isn't to say that the visitor to Afghanistan stands a fifty-fifty chance, or anything like such odds, of suffering so drastic a fate; indeed a party as large as ours was absolutely safe, but it is not a country for the unwary.

One of the easiest things to break on an overland journey, apart from one's vehicle, is the law. To be absolutely sure of staying on the right side of it, one ought to consult the statutes of every country one is going to visit, but this is hardly practicable. The three areas one is most likely to be concerned with are those dealing with vehicles, security and drugs. Each country has its own peculiar way of coming to terms with the motor and the gentlemen who enforce the immigration regulations at its frontiers are instructed to pursue their vocation with enthusiasm. This means that unless the vehicle's and the passengers' papers are all in perfect order one simply will not be allowed in, or worse, should one have somehow already wangled one's way inside, out again.

One trip, with lorries, nearly came to grief when it had hardly begun. The French at Dunkirk discovered that, although they had a regulation which covered lorries carrying merchandise and another which covered buses carrying passengers, they had none for passenger-carrying lorries. We sat around for hours on a cold, wet quayside whilst various authorities were consulted, and it was only with considerable reluctance that our muddy tyres were eventually permitted to defile the sacred roads of France. Then there were the Swiss immigration men who looked askance when informed that we proposed to drive our travel-stained coach, nearing the end of a 13,000-mile round-trip to Pakistan, up and down their Alps on four bald tyres and in second and third gears, first and top having given up back in Turkey. We were only let in because Italy refused to have us back again.

Italy is a most frustrating country in which to drive. One of its chief sources of income is provided by 500cc Fiats; these are encountered at strategic intervals along all the main roads. Other motorists are driven into such paroxysms of rage by their inability to overtake them, because of other baby Fiats coming towards them, that when they do eventually get past it is almost certain to be at a section of the road where this isn't permitted, and out pop the *politizi* and slap on a large fine on the spot. Just such a misfortune befell us on the road to Trieste, and was not helped by a passenger who had drunk rather too much wine in Venice earlier in the day and who insisted on breathing all over the policeman whilst attempting in broken German to bribe him into dropping the charge.

Entanglements with the guardians of a nation's security often arose out of people taking photographs of things they shouldn't have taken, almost always a quite innocent mistake, for it is difficult for an Englishman to appreciate that an ancient steam engine or a policeman on point duty is an object of supreme strategic importance. The camera can also cause offence on religious grounds or simply because it is felt one ought to mind one's own business. I've had rotten vegetables thrown at me in Beirut and been spat upon in Istanbul on account of the camera slung around my neck. It should, however, be said that usually people are only too pleased to have their pictures taken and will stop whatever they are doing and pose for as long as one likes, which sometimes rather defeats the purpose of the exercise.

Not so very long ago drugs moved fairly freely about the Middle East and, although the number of Westerners who smoked marijuana, let alone indulged in anything stronger, was very small in relation to the total taking the overland trail, the risks were not especially high. Now they are and, apart from any moral considerations, anyone who attempts to smuggle drugs is foolish in the extreme for the penalties for being found in possession are severe and rigorously imposed.

One wants to lay down as few rules and regulations as possible for an expedition such as ours. Apart from anything else people who take to overlanding are likely to be of an independent turn of mind and not kindly disposed to excessive restrictions. Providing no one did anything to put the safety of the party in jeopardy, each member was free to conduct himself as his fancy took him. It was our experience that, unless one had the misfortune to be saddled with an extreme eccentric, friction developed between members only when an expedition found itself immobile in some isolated spot for any length of time. Since the point of any overland tour is to get its participants to their destination, stopping only at those places which have something of interest to offer, this situation should not arise. Were the motor vehicle an infallible machine and people totally predictable then very likely it would not. But in reality springs break only too easily on unmade desert tracks; sand and grit get into electrical parts and other forbidden places, and immigration officials take umbrage when inoculation certificates are even one day out of date. Therefore one may fairly assume one is going to grind to an unscheduled halt somewhere along the way.

Some who start out on a journey with the enthusiasm of newly enrolled boy scouts may take offence because they are asked to do more than they consider their fair share, or perhaps because they aren't; either way they end up totally unco-operative. Fortunately there are rather more people who improve under adversity than those who do not.

Assistance when it is needed is welcome, but otherwise it can be an embarrassment. An extreme example of unwanted passenger participation occurred on an earlier trip when one of the coach party became so convinced that the vehicle's brakes were deteriorating into an unsafe condition, despite the assurance of those in charge that they were not, that one night, when everyone was asleep, he climbed underneath and snipped through the cables. Apparently his intention was to force us to have the brakes seen to, but what he hadn't taken into account was that at the time we were in the middle of the Persian desert. Janet was so furious that she hitched a lift into the nearest town in order to have the cable-snipper taken into custody long enough for us to effect repairs and get away from him across the border into Afghanistan. Meanwhile he, realising the magnitude of her wrath and the imbecility of his action, hitched a lift in the opposite direction and was not seen or heard of again until we returned to England, months later.

Anyone who has some knowledge of the working of the internal combustion engine is always useful, as is someone who can speak a foreign language. It would be marvellous if one of the party were a fluent linguist in the various Persian, Afghan, Pakistani, Indian and Nepalese tongues, but this is asking rather a lot and the best compromise is to take along someone who can speak

German. One encounters many people along the way who have at least a smattering of the language, since Turkey, Iran and Afghanistan, as well as many Arab countries, all have strong trading links with Germany. Roger, who had done his national service in Germany, served as our linguist, and a number of us had picked up a few words of various Middle East languages. The phrase we made the greatest use of was *Keile Hoob*, which is Afghan for 'very good' and always went down well in tea-houses.

Tea is a universal drink and in remoter areas often the only readily obtainable one. Englishmen who fondly imagine that as a nation they drink more tea than anyone else are soon disillusioned. Alcohol is hard to come by in Moslem countries, although it can be found if one looks hard enough. While one may be tempted to quench one's thirst with water, it is well to consider the corpses, sewage and other foreign bodies to which it has probably played host, and then forget about it unless one can be sure it has been sterilised. Many of our passengers brought along their own supply of sterilising tablets. They also provided much of their own food, tinned meat and the like, which they cooked over primus stoves. Those who didn't, ate the local fare and usually found it palatable.

Stomach upsets are not uncommon and on a three-month trip one must be prepared to suffer at least a couple of days discomfort. They very rarely develop into anything more serious, but one is advised to carry a basic medical kit. Of course, it is essential for the traveller to be inoculated against a number of diseases before obtaining a visa. Janet and Rachel, one of the other girls on the trip, had nursing experience, which was comforting knowledge, although one naturally hoped they would not be called upon to use it. One of the few occasions any of us had consulted a doctor had been in Kabul on the previous trip and involved Janet herself. She had a cough and had bought some mixture for it, and was so taken by its taste that she swigged the bottleful in an evening. That night we were woken by a frantic banging on our doors and found Janet red in the face and panic-stricken. In between her gasps, we gathered that she had woken up and been unable to get her breath. We whipped her, spluttering and heaving, across the road in her dressing-gown to a hospital, fortunately opposite our hotel. There a young doctor, who couldn't really grasp what was up but decided to take no chances, injected her with a drug which was apparently only used when all else had failed and the patient was about to expire.

Overlanding seems to appeal to nurses and also to teachers, perhaps because their basic qualifications enable them to work in many different countries. Nearly all our passengers were making for Australia or New Zealand, and most of those we picked up on return trips from Katmandu were on their way back again. Some were Australians or New Zealanders, often on a round-the-world trip, England being the half-way point where they would stay and work for a couple of years. Of the few who weren't heading for 'down under' on this trip, we had an ex-policeman bound for the oilfields of Bahrein, two mountaineers making for the Himalayas, and a young American girl, Michele, just out of her teens and seeking spiritual sustenance in India.

We also numbered in our complement Tom, an ex-RSM, who was said to have visited nearly every country in the world. Such a grandiose claim led us to wonder if he might not be a line-shooter, particularly when we were further informed that we need have no worries about his solvency. If by some chance he should run short of funds all he had to do was cable the landlady of a certain public house in Warwickshire and the money would arrive immediately, the lady being greatly smitten with Tom and just waiting for the day when he would cease his travels and settle down with her and the pub.

Apart from Janet, Rachel and Michele, the girls included two ex-WRAFs; two folk-singing sisters, Jill and Heather, and a jolly pair of cousins, Min and Toosie, a sort of female Morecambe and Wise, one rather short and one rather tall, both much given to the giggles and to being nearly left behind.

Janet had calculated that we would need to spend up to ten hours each day on the road, and there would be no relief from

The author and Faith

driving for Jim, Roger or myself, each of us having sole charge of his lorry. What happened when we reached Kabul depended on several factors. If we got a very good offer for the lorries we might sell them and return home. If, on the other hand, the prospects of a sale didn't seem to be particularly good, we would continue with one or more of the lorries, and as many passengers as cared to come, to Katmandu, and perhaps sell them there. A third possibility was that we would wait around in Katmandu until we had collected together a full complement of European-bound passengers and drive all the way back home again.

Selling a vehicle in either Afghanistan or Nepal was always a complicated procedure, and strictly speaking slightly illegal, but the demand for motor vehicles was sometimes such that, by a bribe in the right quarter, the regulations could be circumnavigated, to the satisfaction of all parties—officialdom, the buyer and the seller. Janet and Roger were old hands at the business, but the market for second-hand vehicles fluctuated so wildly that they never knew until they arrived at their destination whether it was more profitable to sell and fly home or drive back with a load of passengers.

So we prepared to set out, uncertain of our ultimate destination or when we should return, our only firm intention being that—following a route south across France to the Riviera, and eastwards through northern Italy, Yugoslavia, Bulgaria, Turkey, and Iran into Afghanistan—we should be in Kabul within the month.

Travel into and through Afghanistan at the time of our journey was comparatively free and easy; since the 1973 coup, however, greater restrictions have been imposed.

CHAPTER I

The Beginning

The journey began on a cold wet March evening in the yard behind Janet's shop. Many of our passengers arrived at Gillingham by train and we met them with the lorries at the station; others came by car, with their friends and relations. We divided the party up among the three lorries, making sure that all the women were not congregated together, and leaving it to the passengers to sort themselves out as the journey progressed, although it was our experience that they generally stayed where they were put. We pulled out into the rush-hour traffic, providing some relief to the usual procession of private cars and Maidstone and District buses, and headed for Dover.

We drove steadily along the M2 through the rain, arriving in plenty of time for the night ferry, and sat about on the quayside. Roger, Jim and myself took the opportunity to tighten the ropes securing the canvas awnings of the lorries where passengers had reported water trickling through. As soon as the sleeping cars of the London to Paris and Brussels night ferry express had been shunted on, we were allowed on board and, with the lorries parked, did our best to snatch some sleep in the saloon.

Our route through France lay past the outskirts of Lille, east of Paris, through the Seine Valley to Dijon, due south to Lyons, along first the west then the east bank of the Rhône to Avignon, and so to Aix-en-Provence and the Riviera. During the first two days many of the passengers prepared their own food over small primus stoves and slept in sleeping-bags in the lorries. The third day saw us in Lyons where we all stayed in a youth hostel close by the river and almost under a railway bridge over which trains rumbled through the night. Some of the party consequently slept badly, but Roger, Jim and I, tired after a virtually unbroken drive from dawn to dusk, had no trouble in claiming our full eight hours.

So far the weather had been overcast and the temperature not much above freezing-point, but as we approached the Mediterranean it became much milder. We had as yet had little opportunity to get to know the passengers, but planned to allow ourselves a short break on the Riviera, spending an evening in Nice and a morning in Monte Carlo where we could relax briefly. In the event it didn't work out quite like that, as my lorry, Faith, began giving electrical trouble which resulted in her being left at the bottom of a steep hill in the suburbs of Nice for the night. The passengers elected to stay with her whilst I went off to a hotel on the front. This was a driver's privilege which could not be indulged in too often, but there would be little opportunity for a comfortable night's rest once we were beyond western Europe and so those of us who were driving took advantage of this luxury whilst it was still available.

We got Faith going again in the morning and under a blue sky drove along the coast to Monaco. There we sat in the warm sun for a couple of hours admiring the view across the yachts in the harbour to the Casino, and briefly wondering, until we received the bill for our coffee, if we were not a little silly in wanting to go any farther.

From Monto Carlo to Genoa the driving was hard going: it was the weekend and the twisting road was crowded with family saloons. Faith, Hope and Charity were not at their best in such conditions, possessing no great powers of acceleration, and we crawled along for much of the way in a slow moving line of traffic. Our intention was to pass through Europe as quickly as possible, in order to spend time exploring the less familiar regions of Asia, so we pushed on resolutely through Genoa and Milan, pausing only for refreshments. But we really couldn't ignore Venice and we allowed the passengers a morning there, long enough for them to sail down the Grand Canal and sit for a while in St Mark's Square.

On earlier expeditions, Janet and Roger had mostly taken the northerly route across Europe by way of Germany and Austria, crossing the Alps by the Semmering Pass into Yugoslavia. Italy was consequently something of an unknown quantity to us and we fell foul of the Italian police on three seperate occasions, once for a minor traffic offence that none of us realised we had committed and twice for being on roads forbidden to lorries.

All the way across the country, it had been mild and sunny but as we climbed up out of Trieste, away from the warm waters of the Adriatic and into the Julian Alps, spring receded and we plunged back in the depths of winter. To add to our discomfiture, Faith became separated from the others somewhere along the narrow, winding road, and in the dark—it was now well into the evening—we missed the turn for the frontier and spent an anxious hour retracing our route through small, silent villages.

The fuel supply was causing concern and we had no liras left with which to pay for more. We made several forays along roads which appeared to lead in the direction of the frontier but which eventually petered out into impassable tracks. Finally, with the needle of the fuel gauge almost on zero, we found the correct turning and arrived, cold and tired, at the customs post. The crews and passengers of Hope and Charity, not in the least concerned about our disappearance, were in a nearby bar aglow with strong Italian wine.

One of the pleasantest discoveries we made about Yugoslavia was that our money went much farther than it had in Italy and a great deal farther than it had in France. Consequently everyone decided they could afford to spend their first night in the country in an hotel, out of the cold, and we stopped at Sezana a few miles beyond the border

The next day the scenery was at first mountainous and then hilly, but from Zagreb onwards for the whole of the afternoon and into the evening we traversed a straight, flat road, well used and poorly maintained, which for the best part of 250 miles presented very little of interest. There had been a few flurries of snow in the morning and the sky remained overcast, the air damp and cold. A range of low, grey hills came into view for some while on the northern horizon, but we saw no towns and few signs of any human activity apart from the heavy-lorry traffic along the road. The lights of Belgrade strung out around the Danube were a most welcome conclusion to the most monotonous day we had so far spent on the road.

The next day, our eighth, was better. Much of our route lay along the valley of the Morava, a wide fast-moving river, swollen with melted snow brought down from the Alps. Apart from our skirmishes with the Italian law and various transactions with shopkeepers and frontier officials, we had so far had little opportunity to meet the people of the countries we passed through. Now, nearing the end of the initial stage of our journey through Europe, we could afford to slacken the pace somewhat. At Nis, near the Bulgarian border, we stopped at a holiday camp which boasted a small night club; there we danced to a three-piece band which made the sort of noises such outfits make the world over. The girl singer wore a sequined evening dress and sang, sometimes in English, in an attractive, husky voice familiar songs by Cole Porter and Gershwin. Had it not been for the wine, which possessed a strange sweet taste, we would hardly have known we were in Yugoslavia.

Staying the night at the camp, but travelling in the opposite direction, was an English doctor from Shropshire who had been working for some years in a hospital in Beirut. He told us that once a year he drove home in his Volkswägen, which on the previous occasion had broken down in Vienna. He had got a local garage to remove the engine and fit a replacement; he left instructions that his old one was to be repaired and he would pick it up a year later when he passed through. He also related hair-raising tales of driving through Turkey, which much impressed certain members of our party until we reminded them that what befell a lone traveller in a small car would not necessarily happen to a group of forty-six in three large lorries.

We were, however, a little apprehensive about entering Bulgaria, for at one time the authorities had been very puritanical about long hair and innocent youths were whipped out of whatever transport they were travelling in, including trains, and later returned to their loved ones sporting an old-fashioned 'short back and sides'. The worst they did to us was to line us up beside the lorries and count us carefully and then spend a very long time poring over the details of each person's passport. It was a wearisome business, but we soon found it was wise to allow up to half a day for the whole party to clear the customs and migration formalities of the country we were leaving and those of the establishment next door which we were trying to enter.

Sofia is a gloomy city, or so it appeared on the dreary wet afternoon when we passed through, the only bits of colour we came across being the varied hues of the tramcars and some picture postcards of film stars, apparently modelled on Hollywood fashions of 1945. Plovdiv, the principal town between Sofia and the Turkish border, made a rather better impression. Apart from the usual quota of monolithic concrete lumps common to almost all communist cities, the predominant style of architecture was considerably more attractive, consisting chiefly of old two- and three-storey houses and shops with decorated façades leaning against each other for support.

We arrived at Plovdiv late at night, at the tail end of a snowstorm, during which Faith had on two occasions all but slid off the road. Once, out in the country, we had skidded into the path of an oncoming vehicle and at the last moment skidded out of it, and another time, in Sofia, had nearly come to grief on a section of road paved with what looked and felt like shiny yellow bath tiles. The lateness of the hour of our arrival in mid March at a town which was hardly a tourist centre limited our choice of accommodation and we had to settle for the Trimontium. This, one of the monolithic lumps, was Plovdiv's most luxurious hotel and really outside our price bracket. But that day we had driven from well inside Yugoslavia and across most of Bulgaria, and the prospect of a comfortable bed, whatever its cost, was too enticing to resist.

We parked the lorries around the corner, beneath the hill on which the older part of the city stood, and left our passengers brewing up. It might seem a trifle peculiar to set up camp in the centre of a European city, but no one seemed to mind. There were a few curious stares next morning from people on their way to work, but about the only verbal communication we had with the citizens of Plovdiv was when a shopkeeper came over to me and whispered 'Bobby Charlton'.

At lunchtime we crossed into Turkey and by dusk we were in Istanbul. In some ways it can be said that an overland journey to central and eastern Asia does not really begin until one has reached Istanbul. For long the capital of the Ottoman Empire, before that the centre of the Christian Church in the East, and still a city of great importance and immense fascination, Istanbul provides a foretaste of the mysterious and romantic Orient. It seemed to us like another world after the grey austerity of Yugoslavia and Bulgaria. Neon signs tinted the night sky orange, and brightly painted cars, buses, trolleybuses and trucks thronged the streets, whilst much of the population was still up and about.

One of the most rewarding and least expensive ways of spending an evening in Istanbul is to wander about the streets of the old city on the west bank of the Golden Horn, peering in through the windows of the shops and cafés, most of which stay open for as long as there are likely to be any customers, and to climb the cobbled streets, over which bright red trolleybuses rattle, beside the walls of Topkapi Palace, before coming down to the waterfront where the domes and minarets of dozens of mosques dominate the skyline.

There one may buy all manner of sweets and cooked foods from the stalls, and a man dispenses fresh water from a large flask he carries on his back advertising his trade by rhythmically clinking two glasses together, a sound characteristic of Istanbul.

A meal of kebabs with a green salad can be especially enjoyable in one of the small cafés which open their shutters wide so that customers have a clear view down on to the street. The small pieces of lamb, cooked on skewers over an open fire, tasted deli-

A ferryman on the Golden Horn, Istanbul

cious at the end of a long day's driving, during which we had been sustained only by *non*, a universal and remarkable stodgy form of bread.

The March climate in Istanbul wasn't much different from what we'd left behind in England. We needed to be well wrapped up against the biting north-east wind which can come whipping down from the Russian steppes and stir the sheltered and normally calm waters of the Bosphorus into a fury. In summer, when Istanbul is hot, sightseeing can become a bit wearying, particularly when exploring the enormous bazaar.

Here the overland traveller gets his first taste of bargaining. In an eastern bazaar one never pays the price asked for any article, and by the time we had been in the city for a couple of days we were prepared to haggle even over postcards. At one time it was possible to obtain Turkish lira in the bazaar at a rate considerably more favourable than the official one. One was not, of course, supposed to, but many tourists did. One simply stood close to the spot where the postcard-sellers congregated and was sure to be asked if one had any pounds or dollars to get rid of. From time to time the police would make a token arrest of a tout and, sometimes, his customer, but this did little to restrict the trade.

Situated at the entrance to Asia or to Europe, depending upon which way one is heading, Istanbul is never without visitors, and there is a constant stream of overland traffic of every sort—oil sheiks and their entourages from around the Persian Gulf, and businessmen from the Lebanon all travelling in large American limousines, parties like ourselves, and family groups from the eastern part of Turkey up for a holiday amongst the bright lights of Istanbul, as well as scheduled bus and lorry services which connect Iran and the Arab countries with Europe.

There is also the railway, which brings people from Paris in two and a half days, the Direct Orient Express departing from the Gare de Lyon, as every reader of Graham Greene will know, at ten minutes before midnight each Tuesday and Saturday. This most romantic of trains may not be as diplomatically and commercially important as it was in the days before the airliner, but travelling across Europe in its carriages of many nationalities, and with an even more varied and constantly changing human cargo, can still be a fascinating experience.

Rail travel east of Istanbul is slow and rather dirty, and travelling on one's own in the more remote parts of eastern Turkey can entail certain risks. However, it is possible to take a train from Hydarpassa Station on the eastern bank of the Bosphorus to Baghdad, Beirut or Baku and, by transferring briefly to a bus or taxi, to Tehran, Meshed, Damascus, and—down the line blown up by T. E. Lawrence in World War I and now being restored—to the Persian Gulf.

A curious, half-breed form of Turkish transport is the *dolmus*, This had the appearance of a taxi, but prefers to think of itself as a bus. It operates on a regular route and sets down and picks up passengers anywhere along it. Fares are considerably less than for a normal taxi—at least they are so long as the passenger makes it clear that he intends to pay at the *dolmus* rate; otherwise, if an unsuspecting tourist is the only passenger, the driver may quickly transform his vehicle into a taxi and charge accordingly.

It is often said that many modern cities are indistinguishable from each other. This may be true of certain facets of their architecture, but it is seldom so of their taxis, and there are few which are more individual than those of Istanbul. We saw none under ten years old and many that were nearer twenty. All but a few were of American origin and, unless there is a vast storehouse hidden somewhere in the mountains where new cars are kept until they have matured sufficiently to suit the Turkish palate, one can only assume that large batches of second-hand vehicles are shipped across from the USA, refurbished with shiny, studded, imitation-leather upholstery in pink, viridian and purple, and let loose on the streets of Istanbul.

Turkish taxis are driven with great flair, if without much precision, and it is safest to assume that they have right of way at all times. Both Jim and Roger had slight tangles with taxis, one trying to pass between the back and front wheels of Roger's lorry, the driver expressing much surprise when he found such a manoeuvre was not on. Whatever the rights and wrongs of a minor traffic skirmish in Istanbul, it is wise to come to a financial agreement on the spot, as a court case can keep one hanging about for weeks, with no guarantee that, even with a clear conscience, one will emerge unscathed at the end of it.

A picturesque form of transport greatly favoured by the people of Istanbul is the ferryboat. This can be anything from a superior sort of dinghy to a quite large steamer; most of them connect the city centre with the Asian shore and various outlying points up and down the Bosphorus and the Sea of Marmara. During the rush hour one can hardly see the water below the Galata Bridge as these boats jostle each other for an advantageous position along the quay; we took one—rather like a smaller version of the Woolwich ferry—when we crossed from Europe into Asia. No doubt the new bridge linking the two continents will bring about a reduction in the number of ferry boats, but many of them will continue to serve otherwise inaccessible islands.

The largest vessels we saw on the waters of the Golden Horn were some white-hulled liners which sailed between Istanbul and the Russian Black Sea ports. We watched a fleet of fishing dinghies anchor just downstream from the Galata Bridge and in a matter of minutes their two-man crews were reeling in their catch; the Bosphorus abounds in fish of many kinds. Most were taken to the markets, but a couple of boats rowed across and tied up to the quay alongside the bridge. The fish were then gutted, cooked over a small stove in the bottom of the boat, put between two slices of bread and sold at the quayside. There was no shortage of customers for this simple but delicious supper.

The most publicised and celebrated of all Istanbul's attractions are the Topkapi Palace Museum and the mosques. Schoolboys in England used to be brought up to believe that the sultan of Turkey was synonymous with the devil; therefore one enters Topkapi—the seat of the sultans' power from 1472 until the early years of the present century—with something of the anticipatory trepidation with which one approaches the Chamber of

Page 33 (*above*) Faith and Hope in northern Turkey the second day out from Ankara—the beginning of the snow; (*below*) Roger and the author in a Turkish village—one of the friendly ones

Page 34 (*above*) Outside St Sophia—once a Christian church, then a mosque, now a museum in Istanbul; (*right*) an Iranian camelherd in the Great Salt Desert

Horrors at Madame Tussauds. Certainly there were gory relics on display; amongst them a gashed and blood-stained robe worn by a sultan who was stabbed to death. Visitors were also shown the path beneath a window where innocent passers-by were used as targets by another sultan whose hobby was firing arrows at all and sundry, just for the hell of it. But the chief crime of the rulers of medieval Turkey in the eyes of the West was their capture of Constantinople in 1453, thus driving Christianity from its eastern capital.

There was another side to the character of the sultans, and this comes out very clearly during a visit to Topkapi. Under their rule, artists and craftsmen were encouraged to settle in Constantinople, which became one of the great centres of civilisation. On display in the palace are examples of the finest treasures from many countries, often gifts from ambassadors to the sultans, perhaps the most beautiful being a priceless collection of Chinese porcelain.

The Sultan's Palace occupies the most commanding site in the city, overlooking the Golden Horn and the Bosphorus to the east, the Sea of Marmara to the south. Behind it stands the most beautiful building in Istanbul, the Blue Mosque. Close by is the more famous St Sophia, a Christian cathedral before the Turkish conquest, later a mosque and now a museum.

The Blue Mosue is one of those sights which has quite defeated the camera, for its atmosphere and colour are too subtle and complex to be reproduced in two dimensions. From the outside its six minarets and domes piled one upon the other are impressive enough, but hardly unique; I had already seen something similar at Edirne, the former Adrianople. It is the interior which is its great glory. I first visited the Blue Mosque on a hot day in late summer, when the cool and silence inside were so great a contrast to the heat and noise of the city that all conversation was immediately stilled. The entire floor surface was carpeted and one's shoes were left outside, so that however many people were within the mosque there was hardly a sound to be heard.

St Sophia, Istanbul, Turkey

It is most aptly named, for the interior is not merely predominantly blue but entirely so, or so it seemed to me, even to the air within it. The shades and patterns of blue and of the subsidiary colours on the walls, despite their vivid intensity, blended rather than contrasted with the blue of the stained glass in the windows to create a breathtaking unity of abstract design quite foreign to anything one finds in a Christian place of worship. We saw many mosques as we travelled through Asia, some very beautiful, but none which could compare with the Blue Mosque of Istanbul.

I was once rebuked by an elderly Turk for going into a mosque wearing a pair of shorts; it isn't difficult to give unintended offence to a strict Moselm over matters of dress and on our previous visit we found ourselves the unwitting cause of what could have been a very nasty incident.

We were travelling into the city in an electric suburban train packed with trippers who had been spending the day by the sea. We were standing, along with many others, paying little attention to the conversations going on around us. Suddenly, farther down the carriage, a scuffle broke out between two men, one in his twenties, the other in his late teens; those nearest to them backed away, leaving the combatants unimpeded amongst the throng. The older man whipped out a knife and pointed it at the other's stomach. No one moved as the train rattled on, although the youth looked pale and frightened whilst the heavy breathing and general demeanour of his assailant suggested he might have been drinking. Stations on that line were fortunately no great distance apart and within a couple of minutes the train was slowing down, and then came to a halt, still without any action on the part of the man with the knife, apart from one unsteady lunge which was easily parried. No sooner had the automatic doors slid open than three policemen leapt in, grasped the assailant and whipped him out, all in a matter of seconds.

We ourselves had been innocent bystanders and were not a little surprised to learn from a passenger who spoke English that in fact we, or rather the girls in our party, had been the cause of the bother. Apparently the man with the knife had been passing derogatory comments upon the morals of any female who dared to show so much of herself in public, notwithstanding that the girls' dresses were, by English standards, on the conservative side, and the youth had spoken up in their defence; out of this exchange the fight had developed.

Confronted by a liberated young woman from the West and conditioned by a diet of cheaply produced American novels and films especially geared to the Middle Eastern market, a young man brought up in a Moslem country is likely to assume that such a female is no better than she ought to be. On this trip, however, we invited no trouble of that sort, girls travelling in the backs of lorries in winter being more concerned with keeping out the cold than following the dictates of fashion. They all wore trousers or jeans and heavy coats in sombre colours, which became more sombre as the going got tougher.

From Istanbul we moved on to Ankara, covering the 250 miles in a day's hard driving. The present Turkish capital has been a settlement for as long as men have lived in that part of Anatolia, which is virtually since civilisation began. It was visited by both St Peter and St Paul, the latter founding a church there, to which his letter to the Galatians is written, but when Constantinople was captured and became the capital of the Ottoman Empire, Ankara was no longer of great importance. It owes its revival to Kemal Ataturk, the founder of modern Turkey, and it is fitting that his body should rest there in a great white mausoleum which is one of the city's landmarks. It is an impressive but not very beautiful building, typical of a certain style of 1930s architecture which aims at being functional, a curious ambition for a mausoleum, and merely succeeds in being rather boring. Our visit turned out to be more entertaining than it might have been on account of a divertingly comic performance by the guard of honour.

The members of the guard—soldiers, sailors, and airmen—were standing about chatting and leaning on the pillars when suddenly a whistle blew; they grabbed their rifles and came

Waiting to board the ferry to cross the Bosphorus

charging past us and rushed down a flight of steps. One of them missed his footing on the top step and rolled over and over until he reached the bottom, where he picked himself up, grabbed his helmet which had come bouncing down behind him, and joined the others in a line on the edge of the square in front of the mausoleum. Almost immediately a column of cars swept up to the foot of the steps and out stepped the Prime Minister of Afghanistan. He was on a state visit to Turkey and had come to lay a wreath at Ataturk's tomb.

One shouldn't infer from this incident that there is anything inherently comic about the Turkish army. It has always been a powerful influence in the country and was much in evidence, even to the extent of helmeted soldiers with revolvers at their waists directing the traffic in Istanbul and Ankara. Soldiers, sometimes strolling about hand in hand, could be seen in every small town and village, and they were on guard beside strategic bridges in the east and the south of the country.

The old citadel of Ankara, built around one of the hills which are such a feature of the city, is now an insignificant part of it. In 1920 Ankara's population was around 20,000; by 1970 it had risen to well over a million. A good many of the newcomers are crowded together in a shanty town on the outskirts, as great a contrast as one could imagine to the villas and luxury flats and offices in which the more fortunate citizens, together with a sizeable foreign community of diplomats and businessmen, live and work. Neither visitors nor inhabitants find Ankara a particularly attractive city; it has little in the way of fine architecture bordering the straight, wide streets of the centre, and in summer it can be unpleasantly hot. In winter the atmosphere is often choked with smog from the low-grade coal used for central heating and in open fires throughout the city, but the glow in the sky as one approaches it late in the evening, as we did, is a welcoming sight.

In Ankara one still feels the tug of Europe, but the moment the city drops away out of sight behind the hills as one sets out for the interior, and there is only a rocky, sparsely cultivated landscape to be seen, then one knows this is Asia. The southern route from Ankara leads down towards the Taurus Mountains and the Mediterranean and the Holy Land. On an earlier journey we had taken that road and in doing so had come upon Goreme, a remarkable city, no great distance from Ankara.

The valley of Goreme is largely composed of sandstone formed from the rocks and pumice powder thrown up by volcanic eruptions. Although now easily accessible, Goreme was for long remote and lay far from recognised trade routes. Christian refugees, fleeing north from persecution, discovered it and settled amid the strange shapes which the wind and rain had created out of the sort, brown rock. They hollowed out caves for themselves, and being holy men they went on to carve chapels and churches, and to paint them from floor to ceiling with scenes from the lives of Christ and the saints. With the coming of the Ottoman Turks to the area, persecution of the Christians ceased and they drifted back to the outside world. In the nineteenth century, Goreme began to attract visitors, a process which has accelerated greatly of late, resulting in damage to the paintings by senseless people who have carved their names across them. The authorities have now stepped in and although one has to pay to visit it—plus an extra charge if one has a camera—Goreme is safe from vandals and worth going a long way to see.

Turkey possesses a wealth of relics of the Roman and Greek civilisations and of the early days of Christianity—the Virgin Mary and St Paul were born in what is now southern Turkey. Many of these sites can be visited by the overland traveller if he is heading for India by way of Syria, Jordan and Iraq, as we once did.

The relationship of the Arab countries with each other and with Britain and Iran is so unpredictable that anyone with a strict timetable to adhere to is advised to keep well away from the southern route, although if time doesn't matter there is much of interest to see, especially in Jordan. But Faith, Hope and Charity's route now lay in as direct a line due east as the roads would allow, far from Arab intrigues and uncertainties.

CHAPTER 2

Ankara to Tehran

By the end of the first day out from Ankara we found ourselves in a bleak, snow-covered landscape. Each succeeding day we drove deeper into first hills and then mountains. At night we slept sometimes in primitive small-town hotels, but more often on the floors of tea-houses. For six days and over 1,000 miles we travelled on snow-covered roads through some of the wildest and most beautiful scenery imaginable. A hundred miles south of the Caspian Sea we reached 6,000ft above sea level and there one felt one was up on the roof of the world. Wherever we looked there was nothing but a vast whiteness stretching away to the edge of the sky. Although the season of heavy snowfalls was over, the snow would linger on the higher ground well into summer. On the road it was packed down hard and from the banks on either side hung huge icicles. Often the sun would shine so dazzlingly out of a clear blue sky that we had to wear sun glasses to protect our eyes from the glare. For hour upon hour we would roll along; Faith, Hope and Charity seemingly the only moving objects in an empty white landscape. In a day we might pass three or four lorries, a couple of buses and perhaps a military convoy, but no cars unless we happened to come upon a small town.

Donkeys were a common sight, as they had been since we left Yugoslavia, their numbers having increased in relation to the motor vehicle as we headed east and now they were to be seen much more often than wheeled conveyances. We encountered a few carts, long and narrow, with a sort of wickerwork awning, and drawn by heavy shouldered bullocks, as often as not in the charge of a small child.

Beautiful though the mountains were, driving through them demanded unceasing concentration, the narrow roads being poorly surfaced, and in places precipitously aligned and graded. The needle-like outline of a minaret was invariably the first indication that we were approaching a town and that would mean an hour or so's relaxation if it was the middle of the day, or the end of perhaps an eight-hour stint at the wheel if it was evening.

Buildings in that part of Turkey were of one or two storeys, constructed either of mud or stone, depending upon the affluence of the district and the owner. Some had flat roofs, some pointed, and there was seldom much colour about any of them. Indeed, the severity of the landscape seemed to have bitten deep into the people, for there was scarcely even a hint of colour, other than shades of black, white, grey and brown, to be seen in any of the towns we passed through.

The women wore long, dark dresses, with their hair pulled back severely and tied in a scarf, whilst the men looked like something out of an L. S. Lowry painting of the 1920s with their collarless shirts, grey or black jackets and trousers, and flat caps. The fez had been banned by Ataturk as a symbol of the old order which had been overthrown; whilst such a reform might seem trivial, to a Turkish peasant it was an indication of new and better times. But a Turk had to wear something upon his head and so the cloth cap was adopted and has remained the peasant's standard headgear ever since.

Another reform of Ataturk's was the transformation of the education system. Previously the average Turkish child had listened to endless recitations from the Koran, which he was expected to learn by heart. Ataturk changed all that by westernising the system, abolishing the old Arabic alphabet and substituting the Roman, and letting boys and girls learn side by side—a truly revolutionary step. Many times we saw children on their way to or from school, or playing; and if, like their parents, they were sombrely dressed, they were far from dowdy—the boys in neat suits, the girls in black dresses with wide, white collars.

The country is football mad. If it hasn't as yet achieved anything very notable at international level, this hasn't prevented the male population pursuing the game with extreme fervour. Partisanship in Britain may sometimes provoke football supporters into excesses of violence, but two of the towns we passed through in Turkey took their rivalry to such limits that not so long ago a series of riots erupted in which hundreds of people were injured and dozens killed.

One had the feeling that violence was never far below the surface. It was in this district that British technicians had recently been held to ransom by revolutionaries and then murdered when the authorities refused to bargain with their captors. The military had been sent in and were still much in evidence all along our route.

In one town our arrival corresponded with a national holiday. In the morning most of the population was parading up and down the main street behind a two-man drum and bugle band, whilst a wild-looking personage stood at a tea-house door with a rifle at his shoulder, grinning ferociously and loosing off shots into the air. This racket was an accompaniment to our breakfast, and continued until a military convoy entered the village and proceeded down the main street. The crowd had to disperse to let the lorries pass, but one small boy failed to get out of the way of the leading vehicle. It was moving no faster than walking pace, but it did not stop and its nearside front wheel passed over the boy's leg. The driver looked down and then back at the road—the only indication that he was aware of what had happened—and the convoy went steadily on its way until the last vehicle was clear of the village and out of sight. A man stooped down and picked up the boy, who appeared too shocked to cry out. Surrounded by weeping women, he carried him into a shop whilst the rest of the crowd stood and watched silently and impassively.

Farther down the street a small bus was parked beside where the pavement would have been had there been one. The remarkable thing about it was that its roof was so flattened that it was touching the backs of the seats. Evidently the bus had rolled off the road somewhere outside the town and been brought in for repairs. The passengers could hardly all have escaped injury yet no one, apart from ourselves, paid it any attention. Such accidents were frequent, remarkably so considering the dearth of traffic in that region, and were usually brought about by a combination of bad roads, poor maintenance and reckless driving.

During the early part of the journey, our three lorries had kept close together, but as each became more of a self-contained unit we grew bolder and travelled more independently, meeting up at lunchtimes or perhaps only in the evenings. Each lorry took on certain characteristics and assumed an individual identity, partly based on the idiosyncrasies of the vehicle itself but principally on those of its passengers. We three drivers, being the only people, apart from Janet, who travelled all the time in the cab, tended to be a bit remote from the rest. Although we had no heaters, the warmth from the engines and the upholstered seats made our lot relatively luxurious compared with the passengers in the back, and we had an infinitely better view.

The only outlook the passengers had was through the canvas opening in the rear and if this was too wide it allowed a superabundance of fresh, cold and sometimes damp air to circulate, and the situation quickly resolved itself into a choice between seeing something of the scenery and freezing, and seeing nothing but keeping warm. The complement of each lorry arrived at a different solution. Those in Charity were a rather sophisticated crowd who dressed with some pretentions towards style—in as much as anyone could be said to when most of the time wearing an anorak, a pair of jeans and heavy boots, the standard outfit for overlanding in wintertime—and were known as the Winklepicker Boys.

Min and Toosie were the only two girls in the back of Charity; they were regarded by the men, when they bothered to notice them at all, as a sort of comic turn. They were always being thrown out or left behind and consequently often finished up in whichever lorry left last, usually Faith. The Winklepicker Boys had a talent for sniffing out any available alcohol and would spend the mornings sleeping off the effects of the night before. Janet and Roger, having finished their breakfast, would lift one corner of the flap and make a rough check of the sleeping forms within before setting off. The only sign of life aboard before about midday would be an occasional bleary-eyed face peering out momentarily from under the canvas.

Those aboard Hope conducted themselves much more circumspectly. The women tended to gravitate towards that lorry, and if the male passengers didn't exactly offer them their seats then at least they might give them a leg up, or down, when getting in or out, instead of throwing them out bodily as could happen to poor Min and Toosie when Charity's young gentlemen were feeling particularly witty. Of the three drivers, Jim was the most dedicated mechanic and was always tinkering about to ensure that his vehicle was in perfect running order. Because it was painted white, it showed the dirt and was more frequently cleaned. Although some of Hope's passengers slept in the lorry, others who were rather more affluent than the general run of overlander stayed in hotels whenever they got the chance. Those in Hope professed to be interested in the scenery and took it in turns to sit by the open flap or beside Jim in the cab.

The people in Faith also quite liked to see where they were going and where they had been. As they seemed not to feel the cold, they finished up with virtually no canvas covering at all, although this wasn't altogether by design. Most of the hard cases were in Faith, and these included the two ex-WRAFs. We also had Rachel, who wasn't at all hard, but got by happily enough; and Michele who was less happy and eventually transferred to Hope. One lad thought the snow so inviting that he went out into it dressed in nothing but a pair of bathing trunks. He romped around for a few minutes and came back saying he felt fine. Suddenly his face turned a shade of greyish green and he keeled over unconscious. Janet and Rachel diagnosed a mild case of shock, pushed his head between his knees and then poured hot tea down his throat; in a few minutes he had more or less recovered. After that he kept his anorak tightly zipped up, however strong the sun, and had no further use for his bathing trunks until we reached India.

Also travelling in Faith were the two mountaineers, Andy and Martin, and Tom, the former RSM, who was turning out to be much less of a line shooter than we had anticipated. He really had travelled widely and had already seen most of the places we had passed through. He was always willing to give a hand where it was needed and had a fund of reminiscences which enlivened the evenings after supper when there was nothing much to do in the tea-house or bare-boarded, whitewashed-ceilinged hotel until bedtime.

For a change we might listen to Heather and Jill singing to a guitar and once, up in the hills around Ankara, we made a camp-fire from wood lying close by, but this was a unique occurrence for timber was either scarce or non-existent. At other times we played cards, including one hilariously childish game called 'Oh, Hell!' in which the entire company could join. The evenings provided some of the best moments of the journey for Janet, Roger, Jim and myself, for then we had the chance, largely denied to us during the day, of getting to know all our passengers.

As a group we got on very well and no one had yet turned out to be a really awkward character, as can happen only too often on such a trip. Although neither the weather nor the road conditions had been very kind, we had made good time, and the lorries had behaved themselves admirably, despite a touch of the electrical frailties on the part of Faith. Since these first attacked her in the South of France, they had recurred, but got no worse, and were contained by swapping the batteries around the three vehicles.

There was one occasion when Faith, Hope and Charity failed to make camp together at night. We were close by Erzerum, the most important city in north-eastern Turkey and, although it lay slightly off our route, Faith was some way ahead of the others and we decided to make a detour to have a look at it. In the event we got no farther than the first tea-house on the city outskirts. After half an hour spent listening to the local music and drinking some remarkably thick and not very thirst-quenching coffee, which effectively persuaded us to stick to tea, we resumed our way. Back on the main road we could see no sign of Hope or Charity and, as it was cold and well into the evening, we determined to stop for the night at the next town and catch the others up in the morning. After a twenty-minute run through a bleak and deserted countryside, we came upon a cluster of lights, drove into the main street of a large village, and parked just off it. Whilst the passengers unpacked their stoves and prepared to brew up, Rachel and I went off to find a tea-house. When we returned a quarter of an hour later the lorry had vanished and with it all sign of my passengers.

I was still standing in the middle of the road wondering how I was going to explain my loss to Janet and Roger and various mothers, fathers, sweethearts and wives, when Tom rolled up and said that the passengers and the lorry were down at the police station. Soon after Rachel and I had departed, a policeman had appeared on the scene and informed Tom that it was most unwise to camp out, 'on account of the bandits', and had insisted that everyone transfer themselves to the police station compound. To emphasise his point he had invited Tom down into the cells and there shown him a captured bandit. He had then proceeded to belabour the prisoner about the head with his truncheon, further informing Tom that the bandit's accomplices were up in the hills above the town and, according to local intelligence, had every intention of coming down one night and getting their colleague out.

We awoke in the morning, without having been disturbed, thanked the police for their hospitality, and drove on to the next town where we found the occupants of Hope and Charity finishing their breakfast. We were now some thousands of feet lower than we had been in the heights west of Erzerum. and the snow was thinning out, although by no means gone. The road was flat and straight and we kept up a steady 40mph for most of the day, stopping briefly for lunch, and just before dusk we came to Mount Ararat.

Often the summit is hidden by clouds but we were lucky and got a clear view of it and its companion peak, Little Ararat. The two mountains rose gradually and gracefully from the surrounding plain, the lesser being the nearest and thus appearing deceptively high and almost equal to Ararat's 16,946ft. The story of the Flood and Noah's Ark's landfall on Ararat seems to be rather difficult for a lot of people to accept, but one wonders why it should be. Most legends and tales passed down through the generations by word of mouth are anchored on a solid basis of fact, and there is much evidence, some of it photographic, to suggest that a wooden vessel is buried in the glacier which is slowly moving down Ararat. Likewise it seems more than possible from the evidence accumulated that the surrounding area was once under water.

Immediately beyond Ararat we crossed the frontier into Iran. The Turkish and Iranian customs posts were housed in the same building and had we cared to abandon Faith, Hope and Charity we could, once the formalities were completed, have passed from Turkey into Iran merely by going through a doorway. The Turks as a nation are efficient, but not, like the Persians, particularly neat and tidy nor concerned with visual niceties; the two halves of the customs post bore evidence of this, the Persian part being in noticeably better repair.

Around noon on our first day in Iran we came upon some of the Russian steam engines which had operated the supply route between the Persian Gulf and the Caspian Sea in World War II. They were rusting away in the desert and we wandered over with our cameras to have a look. As we did so, a soldier emerged from a nearby cluster of huts, making clear by gesticulations that we were trespassing and must hand over our cameras. The strategic importance of five ancient and derelict steam engines rather escaped us and we replied in equally expressive sign language that they were of no concern to us and that we had stopped merely to observe the view of the distant Caucasus Mountains. I very much doubt whether he fell for this but he suddenly lost interest in us and disappeared back into his hut, while we rapidly made off before he could change his mind.

The road south-eastwards from the border to Tabriz, the principal town of the region, was an excellent one. It possessed an even concrete surface, and at one point a series of concrete blocks had been laid along its centre, which seemed a fairly drastic method of ensuring that vehicles remained on the correct side of the road. It took us through mostly flat country, though for a good many miles the Caucasus Mountains remained in the passengers' view away to the north. Tabriz, ninety miles from the Turkish border, has at least 200,000 inhabitants. The city is rather Turkish in appearance, which was about our only impression of it, for we stopped just long enough to refill with petrol and drink some tea.

Petrol was not as cheap as one might have expected in a country so rich in it, but diesel fuel was. This is the result of government policy, which encourages the use of communal lorries and buses, rather than private cars. As far as we could tell it seemed to be working, but amongst a rural population which, until recent reforms, worked mostly for landowners, it could hardly have failed for there were few who could afford anything grander in the way of personal transport than the ever faithful donkey.

The Iranians have been pushing ahead with road improvements and by now it may be possible to drive right across the country on a surfaced road. At the time of our journey there were stretches which had not been dealt with, and some of these were quite spectacularly bad. In places the surface would drop a foot or more and the lorries would find themselves up to their hubcaps in melted snow. Driving in such conditions wasn't much fun for anyone, but if I couldn't avoid a hole I could at least brace myself before we fell into it; for the unfortunate souls in the back of the lorry life was full of unexpected ups and downs. At first they were magnanimous enough to appreciate that the situation was not one over which I had much control, but the next day I became noticeably less popular.

Page 51 (*above*) The magnificent dome of the college in Isfahan, Iran, visited on an earlier journey; (*below*) hand-printing cloth in the bazaar in Isfahan

Page 52 (*above*) Faith's passengers, travelling in somewhat less than total luxury in Afghanistan; (*below*) an appreciative crowd watching the lorries being washed in a river near Kabul

We halted to view an historic bridge which had been demolished so often by invading armies it was a wonder the locals hadn't long ago taken the hint and abandoned it. I parked Faith alongside Charity and, after we had thoroughly inspected the bridge for bloodstains, skulls and other likely relics and found nothing more exciting than bullet and cannon holes, we prepared to depart. Faith had just begun to move when out of the corner of my eye I noticed Janet in Charity's cab gesticulating wildly. I stopped, climbed down, and found that Faith's canvas cover had fouled Charity and been ripped open for a length of some eighteen inches. We did what we could in the way of running repairs and stitched it up, but from then on Faith was rather more effectively air conditioned than her passengers cared for. It was not an opportune moment for such a mishap, for the very next afternoon we ran into the one really severe snowstorm of the trip.

We were making good time on a level track worn by camels and lorries across the desert and, since leaving Turkey the previous day, we had seen no sign of snow, except on the mountains far behind us. Until lunchtime the sky had been virtually cloudless, but as the afternoon wore on it gradually became overcast until I had to switch on the lights. At the same time a few flakes of snow drifted down. We were no great distance from Tehran and the road was fairly busy, so that, although it grew darker and the snow fell more heavily, the lights of oncoming lorries kept us company and there was no cause for apprehension. There were a few hair-raising moments, however, when a lorry, which I took to be going away from us, suddenly loomed up and roared past with a blaze of *red* headlights.

As the storm increased in intensity, so the area of the windscreen which the wipers were able to keep clear lessened, until I was having to stop every few minutes and get out and unclog them. In the back the passengers were huddled together, trying without much success to escape the snow which crept in through the slit in the canvas and swirled about them. It was whilst I was clearing the windscreen yet once more that it occurred to

Tom, whose turn it was to sit with me in the cab, that we hadn't seen another vehicle for some while. Perhaps they had all taken shelter, though it seemed unlikely for there had been nothing but desert for some hours. It would have been foolish for us to stop and let the storm pass, as we had no way of telling how long this might take nor how deep we were in the desert; if night overtook us we should really be in trouble.

So we struggled on, apparently the only vehicle on what had a few miles back been a busy road, and then Tom shouted that he could see lights away to his left. Shortly there were more, moving. I swung the wheel over and we bounced across the desert and found Hope and Charity. Somewhere behind us the track had changed direction slightly without our noticing it and we had continued to hold our former course, which had gradually taken us away from the main traffic stream and farther into the desert. The snow was now falling less heavily and it was this fact which had enabled us to see the lights of Hope and Charity. Although the storm quickly passed, night had now descended and there was no telling in what godforsaken spot we might have fetched up had we gone our own way for much longer.

With the lifting of the storm clouds the sky was as clear as it had been in the morning, but now it was deep black and lit by an infinitely greater number of stars than one ever sees in an English sky. In the desert on such a cloudless night the great arch of the Milky Way was clearly visible. One began to appreciate the immeasurable depth of the night sky and the enormous distance between even the nearest star and Earth, and to understand how inconsequential a pinpoint of light our planet must seem. Far from being overcome with a feeling of loneliness, one felt that one was part of a world beyond one's comprehension, the existence of which the stars faintly hinted at. It was easy to appreciate why men living far from cities amongst such vast spaces and familiar with such sights never doubt the existence of a God.

Passing a Tehran–Istanbul bus in northern Turkey

CHAPTER 3

Tehran to Herat

Among Tehran's great attractions are its streets. These are wide and clean, lined with trees and with water flowing down either side between the pavements and the roadway. Strictly speaking these streams are open sewers, but whenever we saw them they looked remarkably clean and provided a pleasant contrast to the barren, largely waterless terrain to which we had grown accustomed since entering Asia. Tehran stands more than 3,500ft above sea level so that, even in summer, the nights can be cold and many of our party accepted with alacrity the opportunity to sleep for a couple of nights in a centrally heated hotel bedroom.

Once our accommodation was settled, we hurried around to the British Embassy to collect our mail, the first we had received since starting the journey and the last we should get until we arrived in Kabul. For the first few days of our trip most of the passengers had zealously sent cards home, but as we progressed airmail costs rose steeply and the postal authorities along the way were able to relax. On a journey such as ours, British embassies can be a pleasant reminder of home, where one can sit and read of the doings of badgers in Shropshire in a six-month-old *Country Life* against a background of well-modulated English voices. In Tehran, the British Embassy is admirably situated in the city centre, adjacent to staff residences and surrounded by spacious gardens, the whole protected by a high wall. In former days the British virtually ran the country and no doubt had little trouble in locating the embassy in such a choice situation.

Tehran is a relatively modern city, having been nothing more than a village until the end of the eighteenth century. It has grown rapidly since the outbreak of World War II, when it became of great strategic importance on the supply route from the Persian Gulf to the Russian border. Between 1939 and 1945 it doubled in size and is now home to one tenth of all Iranians. One of its principal buildings is the palace of the Shah, Mohammed Reza, the present holder of a title which goes back over 2,500 years. No visitor to Iran can fail to be aware of the reverence felt by both the ordinary people and officialdom for the Shah and his queen, pictures and statues of whom are to be seen in homes, cafés, shops and offices in towns and villages throughout the country. One of our previous visits to Tehran coincided with the Shah's birthday and the city was ablaze with decorations; taxi drivers decked out their cabs with bunting and embellished their windscreens and radiator grilles with pictures of the Shah. Many towns possess a statue of him on horseback, each one so similar to the others that one suspects there must be a foundry somewhere producing nothing else.

Since the stormy days of the 1940s when Mohammed Reza succeeded to the throne and when the oil installations were nationalised, Iran's international relations have been relatively uneventful, a situation which has enabled the Shah and his government to introduce a variety of reforms resulting in an all-round rise in the standard of living. A stable, if hardly democratic government has brought benefits to Iran which are immediately obvious, particularly to the traveller who enters the country from one of its more unsettled Arab neighbours. On our previous visit we had crossed over into Iran from Iraq and, even though this meant that we merely passed from one piece of desert into the next, somehow the Iranian bit looked neater, tidier, less harassed and more usefully employed. Our second day in Persia during that journey had presented us with a remarkable spectacle. We had camped at the foot of the Zagros Mountains and awoke in the early dawn to the sound of animal bells and shuffling feet. Sitting up in our sleeping-bags we found ourselves in the middle of the annual migration of a nomadic tribe which was making its way down from the heights to spend the winter on the plains around the Persian Gulf. The procession extended as far up the road into the mountains as one could see—men, women, children, horses and donkeys. The animals carried large packs of tents and carpets, often with a small child bouncing about on top, whilst in and out of the cavalcade ran the older children. The adults walked alongside—the men had lined brown faces, wore jackets made from skins and carried rifles; the women were dressed in blouses and long patchwork skirts which reached to the ground. Just when it seemed the procession had come to an end, another group would emerge out of the mountains, and for all of three-quarters of an hour the nomads continued past us. Such an unexpected introduction to a country inevitably leaves an impression, and when two days later we had come to Isfahan and discovered its especial delights our affection for Iran was confirmed.

Like many Middle Eastern cities Isfahan is essentially a patch of green in a brown desert and that alone favourably disposes the overland traveller towards it. The tourist who arrives by air, having spent the night in an international hotel and lived off airline food, can have little idea of the joy the overlander feels as he catches his first glimpse of the trees and minarets showing above the rooftops, after spending days in the desert and the mountains, on a diet of tinned meat and vegetables, and tomato-soup-coloured tea made with powdered milk.

Isfahan, like Istanbul, is a city of mosques. It too was once a capital, but it is far from the sea, built entirely on the level, and little influenced by the West. The chief feature of its mosques is their colour—a clear, brilliant azure, so fresh and sparkling that it is difficult to believe that much of it has been dazzling the eyes of visitors and citizens for over 300 years. In corners of the mosques one may come across groups of venerable old gentlemen with long, flowing beards, squatting on the ground chanting the Koran. They are not priests but students, who spend all their lives studying some aspect of the Prophet's teaching.

Hardly a day of our stay in Isfahan had gone by without a visit to the bazaar, which was so enormous that we never really fully worked out its geography and were content to wander through the long, covered arcades until we eventually found ourselves back in the open. Apart from all the usual necessities, ranging from 'High Life' sauce to down-at-heel clogs and op art dress material, the bazaar at Isfahan had a few specialities which lifted it into a class of its own. Isfahan is one of the great silver producing centres of the world and within the bazaar were many examples of the silversmith's art. Like everything else, these could be bargained for and, although none of us were in a position to even ask the prices of some of the more exotic pieces, we were able to acquire sets of delicately embossed teaspoons, and similar small items, for a few shillings.

Most of the stallholders had a few words of English and most of us could speak the odd Arabic phrase and write Arabic numbers, so with a combination of signs, sounds and scribblings on bits of paper we managed to communicate in a perfectly satisfactory manner. The method generally adopted in negotiating in the bazaar was to offer exactly half the price asked. This would initially produce an incredulous smile and a sad shake of the head, and one would walk away. Nine times out of ten when one was almost out of earshot—which if one was anywhere near the section where the pots and pans were manufactured was a matter of but a few paces owing to the din of dozens of hammers walloping saucepans and kettles into shape—one would be recalled with an offer of a slightly reduced price. The real bargaining would then begin and eventually be concluded at a price approximately half-way between the original figures.

The second great industry of Isfahan is textile manufacture. We were introduced to this by way of a camel going around in small circles blindfold just off the bazaar. He did this for a career, which was a steady one if without much prospect of promotion. The purpose of his gyrations was to grind down the dye to make the colours for the wool, and he did this by means of a large circular stone which he dragged round and round. The camel had frequent rest periods, when his blindfold, worn to prevent him becoming giddy and falling into the dye, was removed. He appeared to be well treated and belied the reputation of his kind for cantankerous behaviour by exhibiting the greatest affability towards strangers, baring his teeth at them in a not totally convincing grimace, and showing a positive passion for his master, whose face he frequently licked, to its owner's obvious delight.

When the dyes had been ground to a sufficient fineness they were poured into large vats, in which a solution had been prepared, and stirred until they were the correct consistency to receive the skeins of wool. These skeins were stained vivid red, blue, purple, golden yellow or green, and hung up to dry on wooden poles on the rooftops of the bazaar—the rows of brilliant colours dotting the skyline, watched over by small boys dressed in long nightshirts.

Also practised in the upper regions of the bazaar, on balconies and rooms leading off them and open, as far as we could tell, to inspection by anyone sufficiently curious to look, was the printing of materials. Each piece of cloth was printed by hand, the printer squatting on the floor of the workroom, surrounded by his designs carved out of wooden blocks. These designs, which had hardly altered since the seventeenth century, were chiefly representations of polo matches, battles and hunting scenes, although there were one or two abstract motifs. Delicately drawn and finely coloured, they were beautiful examples of traditional Persian art.

The main exit from the bazaar opens out on to the Imperial Square, the heart of the city. The square is now an ornamental garden, but in its long history it has been put to many uses. At the end of the sixteenth and the beginning of the seventeenth centuries, during the reign of the splendid Shah Abbas, when Isfahan was the capital of the Persian Empire and at the peak of its importance, the Imperial Square became the home of polo, the country's national sport. This was the period when the finest mosques, and many secular buildings, were erected.

Two sides of the square are occupied by mosques, the Masjid-i-Shah, all green and blue mosaic, and the smaller but beautiful Lotfollah, which has a particularly fine dome. On the third side is the main entrance to the bazaar, and on the fourth is the Ali-Kapi Palace. This building, originating in the time of Tamburlaine but much modified, had by Shah Abbas's day become a pavilion from which the court might view the polo. Ali-Kapi has something of the air of a very superior Victorian bandstand, with its ornate awning supported by elegant pillars, but its style and decoration are essentially Persian. The citizens treated the Imperial Square with an easy familiarity, housewives doing their washing in the water running round the perimeter whilst small children splashed about beside them.

Isfahan is the favourite attraction for visitors to Iran, but on this trip it was for Meshed that Faith, Hope and Charity were bound. Meshed is principally the goal of pilgrims and, after Mecca, the most holy city of Islam. It is 300 miles from Tehran and separated from it by the Great Salt Desert. Some of us had previously made the journey in a Persian bus, driven virtually non-stop and with such verve that we arrived in twenty hours, the driver then insisting that one of the girls in the party should immediately accompany him on a tour of Meshed on the back of his motorcycle. Neither Roger, Jim nor myself felt we should try to emulate the Persian coach driver's time for the course, but we saw no reason why our progress should not be fairly speedy and serene; in the event it was neither, a leaky radiator in Faith proving so troublesome that the journey stretched itself out to four days.

Faith had first sprung a leak before we reached Tehran, on the night we were caught in the snowstorm. We had taken her down to the 'Street of a Thousand Repair Shops' in the capital, where one could purchase anything in the way of motoring accessories from Morris Minor ashtrays to dickey seats for Model T Fords. Most cities east of the Bosphorus possess such quarters, their open-fronted shops piled high with what in western Europe would be considered junk but in Asia may be precisely what it needed to squeeze a few hundred more miles out of a decrepis vehicle.

We had selected a likely looking establishment, where the

owner and his assistant emerged from under a pile of bakerlite dashboards, and in a few minutes Faith's front end was exposed to all and sundry in the middle of the street. The offending section of the radiator was cut away and sealed; the radiator reassembled, filled with water and pronounced sound, and in not much over an hour Faith was roadworthy again. We had two days of driving around the streets of Tehran to test her out, and everything functioned perfectly; but once out on the poorly surfaced desert road it had been a different matter.

At the first stop for a brew-up a sizeable puddle had collected under Faith where no water was meant to be, and although we had topped her up, by evening she was almost dry again. We managed to find a local handyman who tried to effect a cure, but without much success; within an hour of setting out next morning Faith's waterworks were spurting forth again. By rights, water should have been conspicuous by its absence, but this was not at all the usual sort of desert and positively abounded with streams. We had managed to keep going by filling up jerrycans at every opportunity and emptying their contents into Faith at frequent intervals, but it was a tedious business and our progress, in a series of fits and starts, was not very great.

On the third day we summoned help from a village blacksmith, who with some primitive tools temporarily staunched the flow. He was most reluctant to accept payment for his work, but we eventually got him to take an ex-RAF tunic which had been rolled up at the bottom of Roger's holdall. Our arrival in the village and the mechanical tinkerings with Faith attracted a great crowd of children. Janet took a fancy to them and produced a tattered old teddy bear and a couple of dolls, which she had intended for the children of a friend in Kabul, and handed these to the three smallest. So shy were they that we had the greatest difficulty in persuading them to accept the gifts. Probably they had never seen such wonders in their lives, for the older children looked on in awe, and the little ones were almost beside themselves with delight when finally convinced that the toys were theirs to keep.

It seemed that Faith's radiator troubles were incurable for she was soon liberally watering the desert. A wind had sprung up, and about eleven o'clock in the morning the tear in Faith's canopy, held together by string, again began to open. I was faced with a considerable dilemma for the faster I drove the more fiercely the wind tore at the canvas, but we were now out in an area of the desert where the streams had dried up. Whether I drove slowly or quickly the water leaked away at the same steady rate, so I really had no choice but to press my foot hard down on the accelerator and hope we would come upon water before we ran totally dry. Meanwhile, the canvas slowly ripped to pieces around the huddled figures of my unfortunate passengers.

We found water, just in time, but so great was the leak that we decided it would be better to tow Faith. Charity was equipped with a cable, wrapped round a winch; we unwound this, attached it to Faith, and started off. Owing to the poor surface of the road and the consequent uneven tension which threatened to snap the cable with every jarring lurch, our speed had to be kept so low that, despite the frequent replenishment stops, it was obvious Faith would make more progress under her own power. After a few miles we stopped beside a large, crumbling mud-walled fort and started to wind in the cable. The site was an inhospitable one, deserted save for some sheep, with the wind cutting into us round the corners of the fort, the sky overcast and dusk fast approaching. We then found that the cable was stuck.

The constant jerking had got it into a terrible tangle, causing the winding mechanism to seize. We had to crawl underneath Charity, where the wind whistled even more bitingly, bringing with it miniature dust clouds, and take it in turns to work away with a jemmy, disentangling inch by inch the 100ft oily cable, whilst another of us held the end and slowly pulled it out across the road. It was dark long before we got the last twist straightened and we had to work by the light of torches. When the job was done, we set up camp against the walls of the fort, leaving until the morning the question of what to do about Faith.

We put it to her passengers that they transfer out of their

roofless conveyance and squeeze themselves into either Hope or Charity, where extra room would be made by moving all the luggage into Faith. The lorry would continue under her own power, loaded down with jerrycans full of water. In this way, we hoped to struggle on to the Afghan border and thence to Herat, a distance of some 150 miles. There we would have one more go at fixing the radiator.

But Faith's passengers would have none of it. They had come this far in a vehicle they now regarded as their own and would stay in her until she reached Kabul. They salvaged enough canvas to cover the front third of the awning, which would keep out most of the wind and rain, and if it didn't, they said, they could always get into their sleeping-bags. So we continued on our way and it turned out that in one respect Faith was now preferable to the other two. Where the roads were dry a quantity of dust was whipped up and trapped inside the lorries; consequently at the end of the day everyone, apart from the lucky few in the cabs, emerged covered in a layer of yellowish brown grit. The occupants of Faith not only escaped this hazard, but declared that when the sun was out riding in her was quite delightful.

Andy and Martin, the two mountaineers, sat beside me in the cab, ready to dash out and refill the jerrycans whenever we sighted water. We had to cut out Meshed from our itinerary, but took a brief look at the tomb of Omar Khayyám, which lay directly on our route. We spent half an hour admiring the elegant monument set amongst well laid out gardens, but our minds were not really on the celebrated poet, being more occupied with the chances of getting Faith across the border into Afghanistan, and we soon took to the road again. We spent the night at Torbat-e-Jam and at lunchtime the following day reached the frontier at Tyerbad.

It took an awfully long time to get into Afghanistan not because the Afghanis didn't want us or were particularly mindful of the formalities, but because they saw no reason to hurry, and therefore didn't, pausing frequently for tea, which we were invited to share. Jim and I declined, and took the opportunity to dismantle Faith's radiator once again. We removed a large section of piping from around the diseased area, then packed the hole tightly with a mixture of glue, papier maché, foam rubber and chewing-gum. Back at Torbat we had bought a number of packets of gum and our passengers had obligingly chewed it to an ideal consistency. Then we gingerly lifted the radiator back into position, half expecting the soggy concoction to fall out all over us, but it held. After we had reconnected the pipes, we started up the engine and left it ticking over in order to give the whole thing a chance to dry out.

Andy near Herat, Afghanistan

Cleared at last of customs and immigration, and with our jerrycans full, we proceeded circumspectly into Afghanistan. The first time I had crossed from Iran my conveyance was quite the largest lorry I had ever travelled in. It was a Persian-owned and American-built Mack, whose high, upright canvas-roofed cab gave it the appearance of a left-over from the 1920s, although it was in fact quite up to date. The road was then completely unmade, to the extent that in a number of places it shot straight down a river bank, across the dried-up bed and came up the other side. On these occasions our Persian driver would throw his hands in the air and bellow, 'Afghanistan!' in a most expressive tone, and then play a tune on his gearbox, which seemed to possess an unlimited number of gears. But now an excellent road built by the Americans has removed the tribulation—and the adventure—from the Torbat–Herat passage, and Faith and her curious radiator went smoothly on their way. Not a drop more water was spilt for the remainder of the journey, the makeshift repair holding out all the way to Kabul.

CHAPTER 4

Herat to Kabul

Herat is one of the four principal cities of Afghanistan and was once its capital. In the sixteenth century it could claim to be the most splendid city in Asia and, whilst it is hardly that today, relics of its great past can be seen. The first of these which the visitor approaching from across the Iranian border comes upon are four, tall minarets. These are visible from a long way off in the desert, and look for all the world like slightly twisted factory chimneys standing in apparent isolation. They are actually all that exists of a once enormous *madrassa*, or religious college. A fair portion of this remained until the nineteenth century, when the British, intent on a clear aim for their cannon in the direction of the Russian army, which never materialised, razed all but the elaborately decorated and now weather-beaten minarets.

The city's chief form of transport is the *tonga*, a pony and trap. In many parts of Asia the *tonga* is a rather ramshackle affair, insecurely borne up by a pair of wheels subject to unexpected variations in alignment, and drawn by bony, flea-bitten animals, but those in Herat are real aristocrats. The traps are beautifully looked after, with varnished woodwork and shining metal, whilst the ponies are well groomed and sleek. The whole ensemble presents a most attractive appearance as it moves along the street to the jingling of bells hung around the pony's neck. In other respects Herat was not one of the most spick and span cities, and there was dust everywhere.

As soon as we stopped in the main street our passengers headed straight for the nearest fur shop and commenced bargaining for the sheepskin coats for which Afghanistan is famous. It used to be possible to get one for as little as £4, and on my previous visit to Kabul I had an ankle-length coat made for £10; but one always took a chance for sometimes an Afghan coat could smell quite as richly as the animal from which it was made. I was lucky, for my coat, which was very warm and proved invaluable on this journey, was reasonably well cured and merely gave off a pleasantly nostalgic whiff of Afghanistan. Jim, on the other hand, had one which was so pungent that half the citizens of Barnet would turn green when he went into the local supermarket on a wet day; eventually his mother insisted he tether it to a post at the bottom of the garden, where it slowly mouldered away.

For an Afghani, outdoor dress consisted of a long coat worn over a pair of baggy trousers, and either sandals or very down-at-heel laceless, lace-up shoes, the outfit topped off by caracul hat or a turban. There was little colour about any of this, various shades of brown and grey being the rule. The main street of Herat was full of such gentlemen going about their business and leaving us to get on with ours. This indifference to our presence came as rather a relief after two weeks of playing the lead in the small towns and villages of Turkey and Iran, but then a city which had seen Alexander the Great and Ghengis Khan go by was hardly likely to gasp with amazement at a harmless-looking bunch of dusty, motorised nomads.

After a couple of hours in Herat, we departed down the main street and along an avenue of trees until we reached a newly laid concrete road, with a quality of surface superior to anything we had experienced since leaving Italy. It was a gift from Russia, one of many we were to come across during our stay in the country. The next one was a hotel, quite on its own in the middle of the desert, complete with a swimming pool, with no water, and a large kitchen full of expensive-looking cooking apparatus, with no electricity.

By now we were beginning to wonder if someone was having someone else on. The amount of traffic we had seen hardly seemed to justify the cost of the road's construction, and now here was this ridiculous hotel which the Russians had apparently

Page 69 (*above*) Afghani children in Paghman near Kabul; (*below*) an Afghan tea-house below the Latterban Pass

Page 70 (*left*) Two of the four minarets outside Herat, Afghanistan

(*right*) the Latterban Pass, Afghanistan

decided just had to be erected in the middle of the Afghan desert. We inquired of the Afghani who some ten minutes after our arrival came padding into the besofaed foyer if there was any food to be had. He gave us to understand that if we didn't mind waiting he might be able to rustle up some kebab. The wait proved to be considerable, so we took a stroll around the grounds and discovered that the hotel wasn't totally isolated there being an annexe in the shape of a small shack. Inside it were the Afghani, a stove, several skewers of kebab, and four overlanders halfway through their tea. One of them looked up and said, 'If you'd come round here straight away you'd have been served in half the time at half the cost.'

We now come to the episode of the miscalculated petrol consumption. It was of a sort which was always likely to occur on one of Janet's tours and was typical of that lady when seized by a conviction that the enterprise was going to land her in the bankruptcy court, and then there would be all sorts of penny pinching until the mood passed. It has to be admitted that there was some justification for Janet's apprehensions, there being several instances of operators of overland tours coming out of them with less money than they went in. We were now in the middle of one of Janet's pessimistic periods and Jim and I were sure that, in her anxiety to cut down expenditure, she had got her figures wrong and that the fuel we had would not get us to Kandahar that night. Janet was convinced that it would and was not to be dissuaded; so, short of staging a mutiny, there was little to be done but drive on until we either arrived at Kandahar or ground to a halt in the desert.

It was now quite dark with no sign of moon or stars, or indeed of anything at all other than as much of the road as was lit by the headlights, and the forms of Rachel and Michele dimly discernible beside me in the glow from the instrument panel. Any curvature in the road was so slight as to be undetectable and the only variation in our progress was a gradual deceleration as we climbed an otherwise unnoticed gradient and then picked up speed down the far side.

As the crow flies, Herat and Kabul lie 300 miles apart; the route we were taking was more than double this, but it was the only practicable one. To attempt the direct route, one would indeed need to be a bird; it is barred by the western edge of the Hindu Kush, a range of mountains which rises to 20,000ft and continues east to become the Himalayas. During the hours of daylight these snow-capped peaks were continuously in sight on the northern horizon. A map of Afghanistan would suggest that there is an alternative road to the north of the Hindu Kush, but although there are no enormous physical insurmountabilities confronting the motorist, the road is nothing better than an unmade track. It passes through country inhabited largely by nomads and is not scenically of very great interest. It is little used by traffic and in an area where the authority of the central government is distinctly tenuous it is not to be recommended for small parties.

We continued on through the night, the steady drone of the engine lulling the two girls to sleep. The distance between us and Kandahar was diminishing rapidly, but the needle of the fuel gauge was hard against zero. That didn't necessarily mean we were totally out of fuel, but we couldn't expect to squeeze more than another ten miles from Faith, which would leave us thirty miles short. We had seen no lights to indicate even the smallest village where we might have stopped for shelter and it was quite obvious that we would have to spend the night in the desert. Although I had slept in the desert before, in Syria and Iraq, it was not to be recommended in Afghanistan so far from any town or village. One hears all sorts of fearful tales of lone Europeans disappearing overnight or being found the next morning—in several pieces. Although probably the majority of these stories have no substance, Afghanistan is in some respects still a very primitive country where the rule of law and the powers of the authorities in Kabul extend only so far. However, we were a large party and the likelihood of our being attacked by anything more severe than chilblains was not very great. Thirty miles west of Kandahar the engines of our lorries coughed almost simultaneously, to no one's surprise—not even, I suspect, Janet's—and we rolled gently and almost silently to a halt.

It was well past nine and the sensible thing to have done would have been to brew a mug of tea and turn in for the night. No doubt sometime next morning a truck would come by, which would let us have some petrol or else take a couple of us with jerrycans into Kandahar to get some. We had more or less settled for this, and the water was on the point of boiling when, to our considerable amazement, headlights were seen approaching from the west and a short time later a bus drew up beside us. Hardly thinking what we were up to, Jim and I grabbed the jerrycans and hoisted ourselves aboard.

An Afghan bus—apart from a few fairly conventional ones operating within the confines of Kabul—possesses several unique features, not the least of which is its seating arrangements. The chassis, engine and bonnet are imported from the USA and are of conventional pattern, but then the Afghanis get to work and construct a body. This is of wood, put together out in the open, usually in somebody's back yard. No two buses are quite the same, but conform to the basic principle that each should accommodate as many people as possible. To this end, the wooden seats are kept extremely narrow, in effect they are simply planks extending from one side of the vehicle to the other; and each row has its own access, as in an old-fashioned charabanc, open to the elements. This doesn't matter because everyone is packed so tightly together that not even the keenest breeze can penetrate very far. On the roof there will be piled all manner of stuff, much of it alive, ranging from human beings to bundles of chickens tied together by their legs.

No sooner had we clambered amongst the entrails of this conveyance than we were hauled out again by Janet who had spotted an army jeep approaching. There was now almost a traffic jam, and we transferred to this much speedier vehicle which was heading straight for Kandahar without any of the detours around the villages which the bus was sure to make. Jim was delighted for the jeep was of Russian origin and he had long admired such vehicles. He vowed to get one out of the country one day, although he hasn't yet succeeded. Many other apparently impossible transactions have been conducted in Kabul by people who have known other people who have known someone who knew the person who administered the regulation prohibiting the particular deal they wished to put through, and who therefore knew the correct spot to apply the pressure which has enabled the regulation to bend the required amount—and Jim may yet get his 'Afghan' jeep to Barnet.

Kandahar is very much an oasis, possessing both water and greenery to a degree which might almost be described as abundant, certainly in relation to its barren surroundings. Long before one enters the outskirts one comes upon an avenue of fir trees planted alongside the road; in a little over half an hour the lights of our speedy jeep were picking out the trunks and shortly we were into the suburbs and being set down.

Street lighting hadn't yet reached that part of Kandahar and it was difficult to make any sense of our surroundings until our eyes grew accustomed to the gloom. Then we were able to distinguish a solitary petrol pump standing in a clearing, in front of some vaguely architectural shapes and opposite a row of single-storey huts. The absence of any activity led us to suppose that everyone had turned in for the night, and we began to think that we should have done better to have stayed in the desert where we would at least have had a cup of tea. Then Jim detected a light showing under the door of one of the huts, so we knocked and discovered we had located the custodian of the pump. He took a look at our jerrycans, turned back inside and produced a handle which he inserted into the pump and cranked our cans full.

So far we were doing pretty well, but we now had to get back to the lorries. Nothing had gone past, either whilst we were in the jeep or since, and as it was well past eleven and there were no pubs in Kandahar to produce a late rush there wasn't really likely to be anything on the road until next morning. However, we took up a token stance and after some ten minutes were surprised to hear a faint rumble down the road towards the city centre, which grew louder as it came nearer, and an old platform lorry came up almost level with us. Our luck seemed too good to be true and so it was for the truck took a right turn and disappeared down a side street, lights and engine dying away as it ground to a halt somewhere amid the closely packed buildings. The silence and the darkness engulfed us again.

From time to time a tiny orange flame flickered further along the road. We walked towards it and found it to be a brazier around which four men were squatting; they moved up and we joined the circle, glad of the warmth. No one spoke and the only noise, other than the crackle of the fire, was the occasional howling of a dog. Then a human voice began to wail. A second joined it, then a third, and then others until it was impossible to tell how many there were. None of the Afghanis showed any alarm so there was apparently nothing amiss. I had no idea what was going on but Jim, who knew about these things, told me it was the watchmen who guarded the city through the night. Each had his own distinctive call, although I found it hard to tell one from the other, and as long as he repeated it at regular intervals his companions knew all was well. Should a voice fall silent then it would be assumed that its owner had been hit over the head with a loaded sock, or had in some other way come to grief, and steps would be taken to investigate.

Our initial reaction was that this was more likely to happen on account of the rest of the exasperated citizens rising up through lack of sleep, but I expect it is a noise to which one soon grows accustomed, just as the inhabitants of Battersea sleep the sleep of the innocent whilst the trains rattle in and out of Clapham Junction all night.

After we had been squatting around the fire for some time one of our companions got up and motioned us to follow him. We entered a tea-house, on the floor of which lay a number of blanket-wrapped figures. There was a space in one corner and though the floor was hard it was warmed by a fire and, as we had taken the precaution of bringing our own blankets, we slept reasonably well.

When we awoke the sunlight was streaming in through the doorway, the blanket covering it had been thrown back, and although it was not much after six o'clock we must have been amongst the last risers in Kandahar that morning. The single-storey buildings we had taken for mere huts the previous night now revealed themselves as emporia, displaying carpets, pots and pans, fruit, nuts, spices and all manner of food and drink. They were doing plenty of business, although nearly all the shoppers were men. The few women to be seen all wore the *chardri*—the most discreet garment yet devised anywhere east, west, north or south of the King's Road, Chelsea. It envelops the figure from head to toe and even the narrow slit for the eyes has gauze sewn across it; an Afghani youth needs remarkably keen eyesight to detect an Afghani maiden's come-hither looks. Until fifteen years ago, when one of the women of the Afghan royal family bravely appeared in public without the *chardri*, it was commonly worn. In 1959 a law was passed enabling women to put off purdah if they so wished and now the more emancipated women can be seen unveiled, particularly in Kabul. But in conservative circles and, as we were to discover, even in some otherwise liberal ones, such behaviour is still considered fast.

The tea-house was empty save for the proprietor who was squatting by his fire brewing tea in beautifully decorated little blue pots, with 'Made in Hong Kong' stamped on their bottoms. He refused to take any money for our night's lodging, but we did manage to get him to accept payment for the two glasses of tea which he handed us. Afghan tea served without milk is delicious and remarkably cheap; a potful, enough to refill a small glass three times, cost the equivalent of one old halfpenny. We said farewell to our host and crossed the street, dodging in and out of a procession of sheep as we did so, to join a group of people gathered beside the petrol pump which seemingly also served as a bus stop.

The Afghan sheep is an odd-looking fellow. Stuck on to his rear where one would expect to find the usual stub of a tail is a great bag-like lump of fat which wobbles from side to side giving him the appearance of a competitor in one of the earlier rounds of 'Come Dancing'. The lump serves the same purpose as a camel's hump and is a necessary adjunct for an animal which spends its life grazing on what appears to be, except for a few weeks in spring, barren desert. As it happened the lumps were of no further use to their owners, for the procession came to a halt behind the shops on a piece of waste ground beside a pool, where each sheep was turned on its back and despatched by means of a long knife drawn across the throat. The carcass was then stripped of its wool, dipped in the water, carved up and sent off to the butchers, a process so speedy that what had begun the morning as a complete sheep minding its own business was by lunchtime partly fried kebab and partly a statistic in the Afghan coat export trade.

As yet no motor vehicle had approached from either direction, although we could hear the sound of engines revving in the centre of the town, and all the while more people were congregating around the pump. Almost to a man they were dressed in the usual not especially scintillating Afghan outdoor get-up, the exception being a gentleman who looked not a little like Tom Jones. It wasn't that he was humming 'Delilah' or waggling his hips, but there was a definite resemblance in his features, his hair style, and this three-quarter-length camel-hair coat. He may well have been a rather worldly Afghani, or perhaps a Persian—he was talking Pushtu—but his luggage, like the rest of him, was not in the least typical. It consisted of a large cage covered with a cloth, which he removed to reveal some twenty tiny brightly coloured birds, hopping about inside. Possibly he travelled the country selling them, or he may have been some sort of entertainer. I would think the latter, for I never saw a caged bird elsewhere in Afghanistan, but travelling entertainers were not unknown. Another we came across was a magician who had worked his way out from Germany in a van painted all over with curious mystical pictures and symbols; this was to be seen around Kabul for most of the time we were there.

Our conveyance when it arrived turned out to be not a bus but

The Mack tanker in the main street of Tyerbad, the Iranian border town. Beyond are the hills of Afghanistan

a petrol tanker. The dozen people waiting at the pump climbed aboard into the home-made cab which had an extra row of seats squeezed in behind the driver. There was even a conductor, who waited so long to see if there might be any last-minute passengers that he nearly got left behind and had to sprint some 100yd to catch us up. He swung up and sat, not on the inside of the driver, where there were already three passengers, but on the outside, where there was only one. This intimate seating arrangement did not leave the driver much room to manoeuvre, but this didn't really matter as all he had to do was grip the steering wheel firmly and head straight for the desert.

Acceleration was slow, but despite the gross overloading we gradually worked up a good pace. We stopped a couple of times at villages of mud huts, which we had passed without seeing the night before, and arrived back at the lorries just as the porridge was being served. By 11 o'clock we were once more in Kandahar, taking on as much petrol as the tanks would hold, and replenishing ourselves with tea, which we consumed in a corner of the bus station-cum-garage. This establishment consisted chiefly of an unpaved yard full of the skeletons of long-dead vehicles, and a few very much healthier *tongas* in for minor repairs. A horse-drawn vehicle stands a much better chance of survival in Afghanistan than a motorised one, chiefly because much less is expected of it. The main east-west highway is one of the few paved roads in the country; the remainder inflict such a battering on an overloaded motor that its fairly rapid demise is inevitable. Although Afghan lorries and buses appear antiquated, few actually last much beyond their tenth birthday. The horse in Afghanistan, apart from its use as a steed for tribesmen, principally provides motive power for the *tonga*, which operates only in the larger towns and cities. More menial tasks are performed by the donkey, whilst the transport of goods over any distance, both within the country and across its borders—unless undertaken by motor vehicle—falls to the camel train.

From Kandahar one has a choice of two routes to the east. In a fast car one can be in Pakistan within an hour by taking the flat, straight road to Chaman; this continues on to Quetta and Karachi. But the traditional route to India is the north-easterly one by way of Kabul; if it was good enough for Alexander, it was good enough for us. We left behind the Russian road which we had followed from Herat—it originates some sixty miles farther north at Kushka on the Russian border—and took the equally well-made American one to Kabul.

The terrain now became more fertile and consequently more populated, and we stopped a couple of times at villages to drink tea and take on petrol. Whilst doing so I wandered off with my camera and came upon the police station. On seeing me, four of its inmates, who were standing around the door smoking and passing the time of day, leapt up, marshalled themselves into a reasonably straight line and stood to attention, all very correct and formal apart from their beaming faces. No Afghani male we came across ever had the least objection to posing for his picture. The one exception was a little nomad boy camped near Herat who, with his sisters, ran like a frightened rabbit back to his black woollen tent at the sight of our cameras.

Our last night on the road before Kabul was spent at Ghazni. The third Afghan city we had come to, and the smallest, it had once been the seat of an empire but had fallen if not on hard times then at least on less expansive ones. In its prime, something like one thousand years ago, Ghazni's rule extended eastwards into India and northwards as far as what is now Russia. Its pre-eminence lasted for 200 years, the greatest of its rulers being Mahmud, who reigned from 998 to 1030 and filled Ghazni with treasures from the plundered cities of India. Virtually all that survives of his great capital is his tomb, a little way distant from the modern city. The rest was destroyed in 1140 by one Ala-ud-din, whose lamp must indeed have possessed remarkable properties for he was ever afterwards known as the 'Earth Burner'.

Our residence at Ghazni could hardly have been a greater contrast to the magnificent structures of Mahmud, being a single-storey wooden affair, which had begun life as the camp for the Americans constructing the road and, on their departure, had

Rachel and four Afghani policemen and a soldier in a village near Katmandu

been converted into the town's one and only hotel. It was full of draughts and bitterly cold; at an altitude of 8,000ft a night spent in a room heated only by an iron stove is a singular experience.

There is little of architectural significance in the modern Ghazni, nearly all the houses being of grey mud, clustered together beneath the grey mud walls. Perhaps the most notable feature is the large open-air market where oranges and melons are sold from baskets slung across the backs of donkeys. Onions were heaped in a large mound on the ground; we bought some to go with the stewed beef we cooked for supper.

The following morning we lined up in front of our respective lorries and photographed each other, and then set off on the final eighty miles to Kabul. For a while we continued to climb, then began the gentle descent into the valley in which the Afghan capital is set. Whilst lower than much of the country around it, Kabul is nevertheless more than 6,000ft above sea level. Just before surmounting the ridge of hills which hid it from view, we turned the lorries off the road and drove them into a shallow stream where we gave them a good scrub, Afghani style. The first time I saw a motor standing in a river I assumed there had been an accident, but lorries and buses in Afghanistan are seemingly as addicted to river bathing as are elephants in India. All the same, our efforts attracted a large crowd which stood on the river bank watching us as we tossed buckets of water over Faith, Hope and Charity. The dust of seven countries was washed away to reveal paintwork almost as shiny as it had been on leaving England twenty-nine days and 5,380 miles back. As for Faith's electrical and water-works troubles, these were quite forgotten and she behaved herself perfectly on the last lap of the journey.

The day had dawned cold and bright, with a crystalline, pale blue sky and the snow peaks of the Hindu Kush to the north standing out against it sharp and clear, whilst to the east the sun picked out patches and pinpoints of green, white and gold, amongst the predominating browns of the city and its immediate surrounds. There was a hint of spring in the air, of green on the trees as we bowled down towards Kabul. The road levelled out and widened, the trees gave way to single-storey mud buildings, then to brick and concrete and stone two-storey ones, and we were in Kabul and at the gateway to the subcontinent of India, little more than 100 miles away.

CHAPTER 5

Kabul

The first thing to be done upon arrival in Kabul was to sort out our accommodation. The choice was wide, ranging from large, very new hotels of the type frequented by well-off tourists the world over, to ramshackle, but cosy establishments which could only be Afghani. One of the most memorable of the latter was the Nawazish, or 'Neverwash', as it was fittingly known throughout the western community in Kabul. Even its proprietor apparently had doubts about its spelling, each of the signboards outside sporting a different version. The implied suggestion that water was at something of a premium within its precincts was only too appropriate. We discovered just two washbasins for the use of the entire, rambling building, and any customer requesting a bath was directed to the public one across the road in the bazaar. At one time eight of us, male and female, with all our belongings, occupied one room, which was cosy, but it meant that, if we were each to use the washbasin at the end of the corridor in turn, the first one had virtually to get up as the last was going to bed.

Arrival at Kabul, Afghanistan

There was little danger of over-sleeping at the 'Neverwash' for it was also a restaurant and, as is the local custom, amplified music blared out from it on to the street to attract clients. Being early risers, the proprietors would turn on the radio at around 6.30 each morning and we rapidly became familiar with all the tunes in the Pakistan hit parade, this being the usual programme. One could hear it at intervals all the way down Jadi Maiwand, the principal thoroughfare, blaring out above the sounds of the traffic, the shouts of the traders, who stood by their open-fronted shops or squatted beside their wares spread out on the pavement, and the general buzz of conversation. The only occasion we heard genuine Afghan music was at a recital in the Spinza, a modern and much better appointed hotel than the 'Neverwash'. Played by three men on instruments roughly corresponding to a guitar, a bass and a drum, its beat was more staccato and its rhythm less flowing and melodic than that which regaled us on Jadi Maiwand.

At the opposite extreme to the 'Neverwash' was the Kabul Hotel, for long the best in the city. Our stay there, on a previous occasion, was by courtesy of Aeroflot, the Russian airline. Our flight out of Kabul to Moscow had been delayed because of thick fog at Tashkent, where the aircraft in which we were to travel was grounded, and after two days of being summoned to the airport every two or three hours, only to be told that there had been a further delay, we began to get annoyed. Rachel, who was blonde and rather good at getting around middle-aged gentlemen, was deputed to ask the Aeroflot representative what he intended to do about our accommodation. She told him that in the West whenever passengers were delayed the airlines always accepted responsibility. This wasn't strictly relevant as we hadn't actually started our journey, but the poor man, who wore a look of perpetual harassment, was eventually badgered into putting us into the Kabul Hotel. There we were given private suites, drank as much tea and coffee as we liked, as well as consuming three meals a day, for all of which we merely signed 'Aeroflot' at the bottom of the bill. After three days of this we finally got away, by which time the Aeroflot man was in a terrible state of nerves, no doubt wondering how on earth he was going to account for it all to Moscow.

The modernisation of Kabul has progressed rapidly in the last few years, but it is still very much a city of central Asia and far removed in appearance from a Western capital. Jadi Maiwand contains much motor traffic, but one is also likely to encounter a squad of businesslike but not particularly elegant soldiers; donkeys which stand all day with huge baskets of oranges, peaches or melons slung across their backs; a man pulling a heavily loaded cart or carrying several large tea chests tied to his shoulders; a flock of sheep heading for the slaughterhouse; a camel train, or a band of nomadic tribesmen striding purposefully down the centre of the street, both the men and the unveiled women vastly more colourfully dressed than the city folk. Kabul, although experiencing something of a tourist boom, gives the impression that, whilst quite pleased about this, it is not going any great distance out of its way to pander to it, apart from putting up some hotels; the pleasant consequence is that visitors can stroll about without being pestered to part with their money.

The social centre for Westerners and overland travellers was the Khyber Restaurant, situated opposite the main square and sharing a modern concrete building with a government department and a cinema. It provided Western-style self-service meals at very reasonable prices and we ate there at least once during each day of our stay in Kabul.

Within twenty-four hours of our arrival the party had begun to split up. Some went off next morning in the little blue-and-white American bus which linked Kabul with Peshawar, the principal town of the North West Frontier, a spectacular journey through the Kabul and Khyber passes. Others flew out over the same route, or on to Delhi, and our party was soon down to around twenty people. Kabul has little to offer the tourist, particularly one who is anxious to explore the more varied delights of Pakistan and India. The open-fronted shops which line the principal thoroughfares are unremarkable, as are the buildings

Page 87 (*above*) A scribe in the streets of Kabul; (*below*) an apricot seller being turned off the pavement in Kabul by a policeman

Page 88 (*above*) A typical local bus on the edge of the North West Frontier; (*below*) a camel train near Jalalabad, Afghanistan, on its way from the railhead at Peshawar to Kabul

within the bazaar. There are many mosques, including a rather grand, newly built one beside the river, but they all somehow lack style. The various government buildings of recent origin are solid, dull affairs, and none of the new hotels are particularly beautiful. The royal palace sits in seclusion behind a very high wall which effectively hides it from view, but there is one very pretty building nearby. This is the tomb of one of the palace's former occupants, Abdur Rahman; it is all gold and white domes and pinnacles and sparkles in the sunlight in a most fetching manner. There are some spacious houses in the residential part of the city, and the British Embassy on the western outskirts is rather elegant in the manner of an English country house.

The chief saving grace of Kabul, however, is its setting. Lofty though its altitude may be, the plateau on which it stands is nevertheless encircled by a series of mountains. In places these are so close that the city has taken a foothold on their bare, rocky slopes; elsewhere they are some miles distant and are approached by tree-lined roads and fields. The city and its immediate surroundings are made fertile by the Kabul River, which is wide, but shallow, and flows through the heart of Kabul on its way down from the mountains to join the Indus at Attock, in Pakistan. Apart from irrigating the Kabul plateau, the river is the city's chief water supply, laundry, sewer, and public lavatory. Such a combination of functions might be thought to be incompatible, but at any time of the day one can lean over the parapet of a bridge or walk along the bank and watch them all being performed simultaneously.

The length of our stay in Kabul and where we went at the end of it depended upon whether or not we sold the lorries. Buying and selling imported goods in Afghanistan is a complicated procedure, fraught with many legal pitfalls, and although Roger and Janet had successfully carried out deals in the past they had always needed the assistance of an Afghani. Invariably this had been Abbas, a businessman they had encountered on their first visit. Although they knew him well enough to visit his house, etiquette demanded that the first approach each time should be made by him. News of our presence was bound to have reached him almost as soon as our three lorries appeared at the top of the hill leading down into the city, and all we had to do was sit in the Khyber Restaurant and await his appearance.

Sure enough, about seven on the evening of our arrival, his familiar stocky figure, attended by three colleagues, materialised at the door of the restaurant. He had already looked at the three lorries, which were parked outside, and assured us he would have no trouble in selling them for a good price.

Abbas was a very sophisticated Afghani. He was in his mid-thirties, spoke English well, had often travelled to Europe, especially to Germany where he had many business connections, and made a living out of buying and selling practically anything in which there was likely to be a profit. We never saw him dressed in anything other than a Western-style suit, and on first acquaintance one assumed he had little in common with the average Afghani, who either lives in a semi-desert village or is a nomad, has never been abroad—except perhaps some little way across the ill-defined border into Pakistan—and has little use for money. Abbas, despite having a wife and several children at his home in the city, gave the impression he was fond of Western women and on our previous visit had ardently pursued one of our party. But it may have been that he was chiefly concerned with the prestige accruing amongst his business associates from being seen with a European woman, for his behaviour towards her was perfectly circumspect. When we visited his house it was apparent that he was fond of his wife and proud of the fact that she had been born in Meshed, in Persia; he regretted that her health, which had not been good for some years, prevented her sharing in his social activities.

Abbas had a very large family, many of whom lived with him. He owned a single-storey house, built around an open courtyard. We were invited there one day, for a meal of boiled rice flavoured with grapes, raisins and saffron, served with pieces of lamb on two large, communal plates. Afterwards Janet was taken into the harem, which is not at all what popular myth suggests, being merely the living quarters of the women in an orthodox Moslem household. Abbas himself may have been unconventional in some respects, but within the harem Janet found a way of life little changed from that common for centuries. The older women seldom ventured outside it, and certainly never into the streets unless wearing the *chardri* and accompanied by a male relation. Although some of the younger sisters and cousins had been to school and could talk English sufficiently to converse with Janet, they all saw their role as chiefly attending to the needs of their menfolk. They had heard of Women's Lib and of divorce and were eager to learn about Western fashions, but had no wish to forsake their life of seclusion. The men of the family were allowed into some of the rooms in the harem, but when Roger asked what would happen if a stranger attempted to enter, Abbas replied, 'I would kill him.'

The furnishings throughout the house consisted chiefly of carpets, cushions and some low tables. There were no chairs; everyone either squatted or lay full length with an elbow resting upon a cushion and supporting the head. There were exterior doors, but within the house rooms were divided off by heavy curtains.

At various times during our stay in Kabul, on both business and social occasions, we were introduced to other male members of Abbas's family, and invariably he would describe each one as an uncle. Some of them appeared to be no older, and sometimes even younger than Abbas. Very likely many were cousins of varying degrees of kinship, 'uncle' being a convenient word which saved Abbas the trouble of explaining his precise relationship with each one.

The obligation towards his family which Abbas felt convention placed upon him, even though the businessman in him could see it was not to his own advantage, is illustrated by his reaction to a fire in the bazaar when the shop of one of his 'uncles' was destroyed. Tradition decreed that each member of the family should contribute towards rebuilding and restocking it. Abbas grumbled about this, complaining that the 'uncle' was a rather distant relation, but he nevertheless chipped in with a large amount. He was having a new house built for himself at the far side of the city, some distance from his present home, and he told us that he would live in it with no one save his wife and his children; he would thus be less tied to the rest of the family, although he would no doubt continue to help support them.

On one occasion Abbas invited us out for a meal, promising to take us somewhere rather special for the evening. He collected us in his two cars, a Mercedes and an Opel. The latter was driven by Medi, his chief assistant; one seldom being seen without the other. We set out on one of the roads which led to the hills, but had hardly begun the climb when the gearbox of the Mercedes started to emit smoke and nasty noises. We had therefore to abandon it beside the road and pack ourselves into the Opel; this was not a particularly small car, but neither was it designed to carry seven. Fortunately we were almost at the promised restaurant, which certainly was rather special, being a former palace with a view across the city. Abbas possessed an almost infallible intelligence system operated by his family, which enabled him to get wind of anything going on in Kabul that might be turned to his advantage, but for once it had come unstuck. The restaurant had been taken over for the night by the staff of the Chinese Embassy, so all we got was a glimpse of the spread awaiting them and a distant view of a dead cat floating in the swimming pool.

Abbas was most apologetic, and also seemed rather upset about the expense to which he might be put in curing his sick Mercedes. This rather surprised us for he was obviously well off, especially by Afghan standards. Roger told us later that Abbas apparently had his finger in so many pies that sometimes nearly all his capital was tied up, and until the next deal paid off he might be rather short of ready cash.

That night we ended up at the airport restaurant on the far side of the city. We were the only occupants of the building and obviously out of favour with the chef, who had been on the point of shutting up for the night and going home. After the meal, which was something less than spectacular, Medi produced a transistor record player, and for what seemed a very, very long time entertained us with poorly reproduced renditions of the 'Glass Mountain' and Paul Anka's ninety-nine greatest hits. Politeness compelled us to appear delighted with these gems, which Abbas proudly informed us he had obtained on his last visit to Germany, and we sat, smiles grimly glued to our faces as he ground through his repertoire, whilst the rest of Kabul did the sensible thing and went to bed.

It was obvious that Abbas's attentive behaviour was partly the result of his desire to put through a deal with us, but we felt—and I think it was so—that he genuinely liked to be hospitable and he enjoyed the company of Europeans. His relations with Janet, and hers with him, inclined towards the formal; on his side owing to his total lack of experience of doing business with a woman, and on hers on account of Abbas's alleged fondness for the ladies. With Roger he felt much more at home and the pair of them got on very well, Abbas confiding in us that 'Mr Roger' was a very honest man who could always be relied upon to keep his word. I don't think there was an implication in this remark that the same could not be said of Janet, but it was obvious he didn't know what to make of her.

Janet was actually very good at negotiating the infinite number of deals involved in any expedition from England to Afghanistan, being quite immovable beyond a certain point and consequently nearly always getting her own way. The only time I can recall her patience becoming exhausted was when we were changing money in the bazaar in Kabul. One could, of course, change money in a bank, but a better rate could be obtained on the black market. The money-changing business was run by two young Afghanis, both even more westernised than Abbas and very charming, but possibly not totally averse to a little sharp practice if they believed they could get away with it. Janet felt that just such a deal was about to be put across her and, looking one of the young men straight in the eye, she said sharply, 'All Afghanis are cheats and liars.' Jim and I were not a little taken aback; the

Afghani said nothing for a moment and then murmured, 'If you were a man I would cut your throat.' We got Janet out of the building as quickly as possible, but so great was the money-changers' concern at the possibility of losing a valued customer that they rapidly conquered their outraged feelings and resumed their negotiations with her the next day.

Although Afghanistan has strict laws forbidding foreigners to settle in the country, we did meet a number of Americans who had lived there for some time and who were engaged on various aid projects ranging from road building to military installations. There are reputed to be as many, if not more, Russians similarly occupied, but they were seldom to be met socially, most of them presumably remaining on their own territory within the extensive grounds of the embassy.

Two of the oddest Americans we came across were Buck and Hoyt, middle-aged engineers who seemed to be in a perpetual state of intoxication. They lived in a modern single-storey house in the suburbs, with a houseboy, a cook, a gardener and a general handyman. Much of the floor space in the house was taken up with three deep freezes, filled with steaks, hams, chickens, vegetables, fresh fruit, cream, and even milk—all flown in regularly from the United States. There was also a great deal of whisky and canned beer. We never found out how much of all this came with the job or what proportion Buck and Hoyt paid for out of their own pockets, but Hoyt was forever complaining that most of his salary went on alimony to his ex-wife back in Florida.

Buck took Rachel and me out for a drive one evening to look at a building site he was working on; Hoyt followed behind in a second car. The two vehicles were in contact with each other by radio and we drove round and round the unlit and fortunately almost traffic-free streets at an unsteady but constant 20mph, weaving from one side of the road to the other, heedless of cross-roads and bends, whilst Buck and Hoyt carried on an inane conversation, each trying to determine where the other was and where they ought to be going.

We eventually found ourselves outside the American Families

Club and decided to go in, all thoughts of visiting building sites long forgotten. We danced for a while to a Philippino pop group, and were then introduced to the 'Major', whom Buck and Hoyt seemed to hold in great awe. He was in his early thirties, some fifteen years younger than they, and had little in common with them. For a start he was prepared to take Afghanistan on its own terms instead of complaining, as did poor Buck and Hoyt, about the absence of home comforts. The Major's tour of duty was all but over and by the end of the week he would be back home, preparing for his next assignment. But he had been in Afghanistan long enough to hold certain hopes for its future, he told us, the chief of which was that the various nationalities providing aid might work together instead of vying with each other. He felt that too often they were concerned with such prestige achievements as the opening of a new hotel or road, whereas less spectacular projects, such as irrigation, were of more immediate benefit to the country.

A manifestation of American benevolence in Kabul, which we personally appreciated, was the USA Information Service library and reading room where we spent much of our time browsing through the shelves. An English language newspaper, the *Kabul Times*, was published daily, and the British Embassy put out newsletters from time to time. Once a week the cinema next door to the Khyber Restaurant would put on a British or American film and nearly all the Westerners would attend, regardless of its subject or merit.

Despite Abbas's repeated assurances that a profitable deal concerning all three lorries would be concluded very shortly, it appeared to us that any such thing was actually far from immediate. So a small party, led by Jim and including some of our remaining passengers, decided to visit Bamian, the most celebrated monument to the Buddhist religion once practised throughout Afghanistan.

The Afghanis consist of several races, chief amongst them both in size and in political influence being the Pathans, Kipling's 'wily tribesmen'. The most easily distinguished of the minority groups are the Hazarahs who are mongoloid in appearance and quite unlike other Afghanis. They are the descendants of the followers of Ghengis Khan and it was he who drove out Buddhism from Afghanistan. Something of the fierce character of the hordes which swept across Asia in the twelfth century survives in these modern Hazarahs, a fifth of whom serve in the Afghan army, although many more live peaceful lives as farmers.

At the time of Ghengis Khan's invasion, the Valley of Bamian was the home of a community of Buddhist monks and contained at least ten monasteries. Ghengis slaughtered or drove out all the monks and destroyed their places of worship, but the valley's most remarkable religious monuments—two statues of Buddha, the largest 120ft high, carved into the red rock wall—defeated him. He stripped them of their gold leaf and rich colours and cut away their noses, but that was as much as he could achieve.

We arrived at Bamian late in the afternoon, the journey from Kabul, much of it over a dirt road and taking in two 10,000ft summits, occupying the best part of a day. Despite its remote position, Bamian is much visited and sports a modern hotel. Scurrying around the valley during our stay were a number of Citroen 2CVS which had been taking part in an overland rally from Paris.

As soon as the sun rose next day we climbed the series of steps cut into the rock beside the Buddhas and shared their view across the green Bamian Valley, which they have enjoyed for 1,600 years. The statues are hardly beautiful, especially since Ghengis's mutilations, but undeniably impressive. The traces of frescoes painted on the surface of the niches in which they stood indicated how richly decorated they must once have been.

We moved on to Band-i-Mir, where another remarkable and unexpected spectacle awaited us. The mountains in the area of Bamian contain an unusually high proportion of minerals and as the rains wash over them considerable quantities of salts are collected. When the waters eventually form lakes at the base of the mountains, their mineral content colours them to a brilliant turquoise hue, the intensity varying according to the depth of the water and the angle at which one views it. We first saw the lakes from some distance above them; their brilliance was dazzling, particularly against the pinkish tones of the surrounding mountains. As more water flows down the mountainsides, the lakes overflow, building up a wall of minerals and salt. The local people take advantage of this, and primitive mills, consisting chiefly of two big grinding stones, are plentiful in Band-i-Mir.

Farther north, but more accessible than Bamian or Band-i-Mir are the sites of two cities raided by the Mongols—Mazar-i-Sharif and Balkh—which we were able to visit on a subsequent journey through Afghanistan, when we took the northern route from Herat. This was not normally used by visitors, both on account of its unsuitability for motor vehicles and the unpredictability of the attitude of the nomads towards travellers. The police carefully noted our time of departure from Herat and checked us in at each of the few towns along the way. It was hard going but we reached Mazar-i-Sharif without incident in five days.

The great attraction of this, the principal town of northern Afghanistan, is the mosque of Caliph Ali. Decorated in blue and turquoise tiles, it is now very well cared for after years of neglect, and not dissimilar in style to the mosques of Isfahan. The tomb of Ali, the fourth caliph of the Moslem world, was discovered here in the twelfth century, and a mosque was erected to mark the site. Hardly was the last pinnacle in place when Ghengis Khan arrived and razed the entire edifice to the ground. The present mosque was put up on the site of the original. Mazar-i-Sharif is a pleasant town of wide streets, situated like Kabul against the background of the Hindu Kush, with the important difference that the mountains lie to the south instead of the north of the town.

Just before reaching Mazar-i-Sharif, we passed the substantial ruins of what was once the capital of a great central Asian empire. This was Balkh, or Bactra as it was known in Alexander's time, when he and his army camped there on his way to conquer India. Like Mazar-i-Sharif, it suffered at the hands of the Mongols and, although when Marco Polo passed through it some fifty years afterwards he found much of it intact, Ghengis's savage assault seemed to have taken away its will to survive and it gradually declined to its present sad, abandoned state. Of prehistoric origins, the site has been undergoing archaeological excavation for some time.

This part of Afghanistan, remote though it is to travellers over the recognised west-east tourist route through Kabul, is assuming considerable strategic importance on account of its proximity to Russia. Mazar-i-Sharif stands at the junction of three roads, one heading north to the Russian border, whilst 100 miles to the north-east is Qizil Qala, a railhead and port on the River Oxus. Much of Afghanistan's long-established and growing trade with Germany is conducted through here, coming by train as far as the Aral Sea and thence by barge. The road from the border to Kabul has been much improved of late, with Russian aid, and includes a 1½-mile tunnel through the mountains at the Salang Pass.

North of Kabul, within an easy distance for a day's excursion, is Paghman, a much more recent monument. It was the out-of-town home of Amanullah, one of the most colourful, if less successful, rulers of Afghanistan. It lies in a green and pleasant spot overlooking the Kabul Valley and is itself overlooked by the nearby mountains.

When Lowell Thomas—the first man to drive by car from the North West Frontier to Kabul—visited Paghman in the early 1920s he was introduced to a Turk, Tewfik Bey, who was responsible for most of the architecture of the place. Amanullah had just returned from an extensive tour of Europe which had fired him with an enthusiasm for all things Western, and Tewfik Bey was one of his protégés. The Turk declared that he had 'taken his designs partly from houses he had seen in America, in so far as he could remember what they actually looked like', but that he was also 'trying to introduce a suggestion of the architecture of Swiss chalets'. The result was a peculiar but not unattractive conglomeration of styles, curiously in harmony with the setting.

Wrestlers in the Central Park in Kabul

A further innovation of Amanullah's was a cinema. It was still intact, but disused and all boarded up. The king, who by all accounts was a rather attractive, if eccentric character, moved far too quickly for the comfort of the majority of his subjects and was forced to abdicate, since when Afghanistan has continued to adopt Western ideas but at a more leisurely rate.

We returned from Bamian and Paghman to find Abbas's attempts to sell the lorries little nearer fruition. A dozen or so of our original passengers were still in Kabul and willing to come with us to Katmandu should we decide to go on. A number of other overland travellers, who had arrived from Europe by various means, also expressed interest in joining us. It was two years since Roger and Janet had last visited Nepal, whilst Jim and I had never got that far, so we all had a hankering to continue the journey, regardless of where the greatest profit lay. We deliberated for some while and finally concluded that we would leave two of the lorries in the customs yard, for safe keeping, and take the most economical of the three, Hope, on to Katmandu. Abbas would meanwhile continue to canvass his many uncles and acquaintances for buyers for Faith and Charity.

There were twenty-four in the party. We had lost all our Australians, but still had one New Zealander; and we had acquired two Canadians and a Frenchman. There was also a girl from Denmark, married to an Englishman, the pair of them being on their way from a kibbutz in Israel to make their home in Australia. For the first time Jim, Roger and I—taking it in turn to drive—had an opportunity to sample the delights of riding in the back of a lorry. We left Kabul early one afternoon, the sun shining as it had done every day of our stay, the air noticeably warmer than it had been on our arrival ten days earlier, and headed east towards Pakistan, which we hoped to enter sometime the next day.

CHAPTER 6

Through the Khyber to Lahore

During our journey out from England we had seen so many impressive works of nature—the Alps, the Adriatic from above Trieste, the Turkish mountains, the Caucasus, the Persian and Afghan deserts, the Hindu Kush—that we approached the celebrated Latterban Pass, a little way out from Kabul, with no great sense of anticipation. Consequently the breathtaking splendour of the rocky gorge through which we descended for the next two hours quite astonished us.

The Latterban Pass has for long been the principal route from the Kabul plateau to the plains of India chiefly because travellers, as well as invaders, have been led to it by the Kabul River, which flows down the gorge on its way to join the Indus at Attock. It was at its approaches that the British army retreating from Kabul in 1842 was slaughtered, the tribesmen picking off the soldiers and their entourage at will from the heights above. The modern, well-surfaced, German-built road for the most part follows the bends and twists of the river, keeping level with it on the less precipitous stretches. Then, when the river cascades vertically down, the road sweeps around the rock face above it before lunging across the gorge by way of a stone bridge and gradually winding down parallel with the river again. From being something of an inconvenience, the open back of our lorry now became a perfect viewing platform from which we gazed upon a succession of startling vistas, the rocks stretching away to such heights that the sky became a small, jagged patch of blue amongst them, growing ever smaller with each twist of the road.

At the end of the gorge we emerged into a very different landscape, although hardly less beautiful. The road led us out from amongst the towering rocks into a wide, green valley of rice fields and to a village which seemed to consist almost entirely of tea-houses with thatched roofs. We reached the valley in the late evening when the sun had sunk out of sight below the tops of the mountains, but because we were closer to sea level than we had been for over a month the air was still warm and there was little suggestion of the chill we had come to expect at sunset. Close by the village was a lake and from it came the sound of frogs croaking down in the reeds at the water's edge. In the gardens behind the houses were orange trees, their fruit almost ripe.

On the mud flats on the far shore of the lake a camel train was settling down for the night. The camels crouched on their haunches with their packs beside them, while the drivers and their families were either inside their black goat-skin tents or stretched out close by, wrapped in brightly coloured blankets, probably bought in the markets of Peshawar. The camel train would take the best part of two weeks over the journey to Kabul; this would not greatly matter, providing it was not carrying perishable goods, but the fact that a lorry can cover the distance in a day inevitably means that much of the traffic now goes by the quicker method.

Almost all the motor vehicles operating between Peshawar and Kabul are Pakistani owned and, compared with those of the Afghanis, are far better cared for and very much more decorative. They are nearly all of British origin, the chassis, bonnet and windscreen coming from the Bedford factory at Luton. The rest of each truck, the Pakistani bit, is a real work of art. The name of the owner will probably be painted on the side, sometimes in old English script, sometimes additionally in Pushtu, and intertwined around it will be bunches of flowers, scrolls and mysterious symbols, whilst alongside will be pictures of trains, ships, rockets, aeroplanes, golden sunsets and the prophet Mohammed, all in vivid and clashing colours. On the bonnet there will be imitation chromium-plated rivets and false hinges, and a sort of cowcatcher affair of chains swinging from the bumper. From the top of the windscreen hangs a decorous fringe of plastic lace, while inside the cab the upholstery, the door panels, the roof and the dashboard are covered in dazzling imitation leather. The gear and brake levers and the steering column are bound around with coloured sticky tape, and the final touch, above the dashboard, is a row of postcards—of Mohammed, a pin-up or two, a view of Istanbul, and snapshots of the driver's friends.

The Peshawar–Kabul road is Afghanistan's lifeline to the outside world. Nearly all its imports take this route, arriving at Peshawar by train from Karachi, which may be said to be Afghanistan's chief port, albeit some 400 miles from its borders. The people who live along the road in the North West Frontier region and as far east as the Indus are Pathans. They have long regarded this territory as their own and there was almost continual fighting in the area whilst the British ruled India, a situation which the setting up of Pakistan in 1947 did little to alter. In the early 1960s this led to a severance of diplomatic relations between Pakistan and Afghanistan. Despite a Russian airlift into and out of Kabul, normal trade was impossible under such conditions and Afghanistan had to back down. The prime minister was sacked and for the first time a commoner assumed this office. Nevertheless the political power wielded by the royal family remained considerable until the 1973 coup.

Our last night in Afghanistan was spent on the verandah of the largest tea-house in the village beside the lake. Like all owners of such establishments, the proprietor appeared in no way put out when asked if he could accommodate a party of travellers at short notice, and room was found for us all. The typical tea-house consisted of one large room, which was often the entire building; others might have additional rooms, sometimes divided from the main one by curtains, sometimes not. The lavatory was simply a hole in the ground in an outhouse. None of us by this stage of the journey was especially pernickety, but tea-house sanitation could be such a vividly unspoilt relic of an age-old way of life that we preferred to disappear into the desert and make our own arrangements. The walls of the tea-house were usually of mud, as was the floor, although this was often covered by rugs or carpets, and perhaps there would be wooden benches. The front might be open to the street, with tables and seats set up outside. Wooden shutters could be pulled across at night to keep the interior warm, but such refinements were mostly restricted to houses in the main streets of towns or cities; the entrance to the typical village tea-house being a low opening, protected at night by a curtain. However primitive its appointments, a really dirty tea-house was unknown. The floor was continually swept so that one could sit on it, drinking one's tea around the stove, which was the focal point of every tea-house and ensured that, whatever conditions were like outside, there was always a warm, muggy and inviting atmosphere within.

At lunchtime the next day we crossed into Pakistan and prepared to view what many of us were anticipating would be the highlight of our trip, the Khyber Pass. In this we were disappointed. We might have been less critical had we approached it from the opposite direction, without having the glories of the Latterban still fresh in our minds; as it was, the gentle descent through a not particularly deep or narrow pass seemed tame by comparison. The weather was overcast, which didn't help, and no doubt we should have realised that the Khyber's claim to fame lay in its strategic position and historic associations rather than in any outstanding visual splendours.

Unlike many previous conquerors of India, the British approached by sea and only arrived at the Khyber after most of the rest of the country had been subdued. They fortified the Pass—against both the local tribesmen and a possible Russian invasion—with a number of stockades built out of the rock. These remain, with the crests of the British, Indian and Pakistani regiments which have served on the North West Frontier carved into their walls. To this day anyone venturing into the Khyber after nightfall takes his life in his hands. The Pakistan authorities forbid any movement of vehicles during the hours of darkness, and at Jamrud, the fort standing at the eastern end of the Pass, the

Page 105 (*above*) On the Afghan–Pakistan border, British lorries with locally-built bodies; (*below*) tribesmen at the entrance to the Khyber Pass, in front of the gateway erected to mark the beginning of the North West Frontier

Page 106 (*left*) The author outside the Taj Mahal, India

(*right*) water buffalo in paddy fields in Uttar Pradesh, India, alongside the Grand Trunk Road

menfolk of the village commonly stroll about with rifles slung across their shoulders. Even during daylight hours one is not encouraged to halt one's vehicle in the Pass, although we did, briefly, to roll back the hood when it came on to rain.

There are two other routes running through the Khyber—a road used by the camel trains, which criss-crossed the one on which we were travelling, and the railway. The latter owed its existence to the needs of military strategy rather than to those of trade and it is now partly abandoned. A train continues to run twice a week to Landi Kotal, at the head of the Pass, but it is no longer possible to journey the final few, spectacular miles through a succession of tunnels to within sight of the Afghan border. As it is, the climb up the Pass from Peshawar is a tough proposition, and the train we watched puffing its way slowly past us was hauled by two powerful, if elderly steam engines, built in Glasgow some fifty years ago.

In many towns in Pakistan and India the station dining-room provides the traveller with his best chance of obtaining a hot meal, and on arriving at Peshawar, an hour's run from the foot of the Khyber, we headed for the European-style dining-room of the Cantonment station. A uniformed waiter welcomed us, presented the menu and showed us to our table. He then disappeared into the kitchen, returning some ten minutes later to announce that the items we had ordered were off and would we settle for eggs? As we obviously had little choice, we agreed and the waiter once more retreated to his kitchen. A further wait ensued, punctuated by a failure of the lights; this was brought to an end by the entry of the waiter with a large tray bearing two poached eggs and several pieces of toast. These, we were informed, were the entire contents of the larder. It may therefore be understood that we were not initially much impressed with railway dining-rooms; but the following day, at Rawalpindi, we tried again and had an excellent curry. After that we were never again disappointed in railway catering, either in Pakistan or India, and made great use of it.

Our departure from Afghanistan meant an end to nights spent

on the floors of the tea-houses, for in India and Pakistan we stayed for the most part in dak bungalows. These originated in the days of the British Raj, being put up for the use of the district officer during his tours of the territory, and when not required by him were available to all. Normally each is in charge of a caretaker and provides the basic essentials of a roof and a bed at a cost of a few pence. There are several communal bedrooms, a bathroom with running water—though this is seldom hot—and, sometimes, cooking facilities. A party of some twenty travellers tended to put rather a strain on the sleeping accommodation. At the first dak bungalow at which we stayed, we suggested setting up our own beds and sleeping-bags out on the lawn in front. On being informed that this was an excellent method of attracting the local snake population, we abruptly changed our minds and settled for the verandah. As a result of these precautions, the only snakes we encountered were performing ones, although on occasions on still nights swishings might be heard in the long grass around the bungalow, which Rachel claimed were snakes stalking her.

We saw little of Peshawar, arriving there late in the afternoon and departing early the next morning, but we gained an impression of lush gardens, their rich greenery interspersed with clumps of red and pink blossoms; of many English-language road signs, Leyland double-decker buses, and military lorries almost identical to Faith, Hope and Charity, and of more exotic sights—buffalo carts, food shops stocked with unfamiliar delicacies, and Pathan women wearing the *chardri*, as in Afghanistan. Their menfolk carried rifles and wore caracul hats or turbans, in contrast to the Pakistanis' attire of wide, baggy white or pale coloured trousers and shirt, with the head left uncovered.

At Peshawar we altered direction a few degrees to the south, having travelled due east with little variation since leaving the French Riviera, and for nearly a thousand miles followed the Grand Trunk Road, the sun beating more fiercely down upon us each day. We pulled the canvas awning of the lorry half-way back so that some shade was provided, but a number of our passengers preferred to lie on top of it and sunbathe. After weeks in the icy conditions of northern Turkey and Iran it was a natural reaction, but within an hour all but Heather and Jill, the two sisters, had had enough. They stuck it out for most of the morning and by lunchtime their skins were beginning to turn a deep red; their heads, despite being covered by large, floppy hats, ached, and their bodies burned all over. They spent the rest of the day in great discomfort and for several more they found movement agony, flinching whenever the hems or necks of their dresses chafed against them.

Towards evening on our first day on the Grand Trunk Road we came to the Indus. As we approached Attock, where we would make the crossing of the river, the road climbed steadily from the surrounding plain, up wooded slopes and then swung south into a narrowing gorge. Through the trees to the north-west we could see a great expanse of water, which was the meeting place of the Kabul and Indus rivers. The sides of the gorge became ever more precipitous; finally there was no longer room for the road and it swung out on to a narrow steel-girder bridge. This possessed two decks, one for the railway, and one for the road which was wide enough for only one line of vehicles and controlled by traffic lights at each end. We waited our turn and then crossed, with the river, swollen by the melted snows of the Himalayas, racing beneath us and down the gorge towards the plains of Multan, Khairpur and Hyderabad, finally to empty into the Arabian Sea below Karachi. We gained the eastern bank and climbed away from the river, skirting the walls of a large fort, and then, on level ground again, headed south-east.

The perennial bane of the subcontinent of India is an excess of population and a shortage of water. Part of the attempt to counter the former was evident in the bright yellow vans each labelled 'Government Mobile Family Planning Clinic'; while an answer to the second was the Mangla Dam. This is a vast scheme, newly completed, to irrigate those areas of the Punjab and Kashmir which were previously only fitfully watered. We intended visiting an English girl, Nicola, a passenger on a previous overland trip, who was working in the dam offices. We turned off the main road, drove some ten miles into the village of neatly laid-out bungalows looking down on the dam and found Nicola playing squash. She was a tall, attractive girl with a sense of humour, on whom we had come to rely during the more wearing passages of that earlier journey and we were glad to renew her acquaintance. We had no one with quite her force of personality on the present trip, our characters tending to be more of the knock-about comic variety. She said she rather missed travelling and to get a taste of it again she came back with us down to the Grand Trunk Road and stayed the night in our dak bungalow, returning early next morning in a local bus.

On our fourth afternoon out from Kabul and some six weeks after leaving England, we reached Lahore, Pakistan's second city and close to the Indian border. Relations between the two countries being what they are, we had been unable to obtain confirmation anywhere along our route whether we should be allowed across. We were therefore much relieved to find that, although we could not continue along the Grand Trunk Road to Amritsar, by making a detour of some sixty miles we would find a frontier post through which we might pass. Our authority to do so would be ready next morning. We booked in for the night in a once palatial but now somewhat rundown hotel on the edge of the old city. One section of Lahore is very westernised, with tall office blocks, expensive restaurants and shops, wide streets and many motor-cars and taxis. In the other part, the motor vehicle is a comparatively rare sight; motor-scooter trishaws are fairly common but the bulk of the traffic consists of *tongas*, solid-wheeled bullock carts, and drays propelled by barefoot, skinny men. The buildings seem to be constructed chiefly of fretwork and look so fragile and decayed that it is a wonder anyone dares venture inside them. Inevitably we repaired to the station for supper.

Apart from the quality of its food, a railway station was an excellent place to meet people; more often than not someone would come over to us and start a conversation. No sooner had

An old woman near Jhelum, Pakistan

we sat down than a youngish couple introduced themselves; he was Pakistani, she was English. The husband said that he had 'a very important job with the United Dairies in London' and generally appeared pleased with his progress through the world so far, but his wife complained that in Pakistan women were treated as second-class citizens and she couldn't wait to get back home.

We were taken along by the husband to meet an old school-friend, the assistant station-master, who turned out to be a tall, handsome man in his early thirties, dressed in a magnificent white uniform; with it went a pith helmet which sat on his desk in front of him. The assistant station-master was altogether less voluble than his friend but, when pressed, admitted that he had once played test cricket for his country. He took us on a tour of his station, pointing out the platform on which scenes from Bwohani Junction had been filmed, and talked of the grim realities of 1947 when trainloads of dead and dying refugees, fleeing from their homes in India, arrived in Lahore.

The station was large, with steam and diesel trains arriving and departing at frequent intervals and passengers crowding the platforms. Away from the bustle at the far end of the station, a group of some twenty porters, shunters and other railwaymen was assembled in several ranks, facing south-westwards. At regular intervals, without any apparent word of command, the men would prostrate themselves, their foreheads touching the ground, oblivious of the trains rumbling past a few feet away. The assistant station-master appeared surprised that we should remark upon the sight, explaining that they always made their religious observances at that hour and their duties prevented them attending the mosque.

Rachel and I took a trishaw back to the hotel; although it was now well into the evening, the volume of traffic had hardly decreased since the rush-hour. We weaved in and out of the slowly moving stream of vehicles, which at every intersection closely resembled a lethargically spinning whirlpool as each jockeyed for position. There was hardly even a token recognition of the rule of the road, our driver veering from one side to the other, dodging pedestrians who likewise paraded where their fancy took them, and on a couple of occasions circumnavigating a double-decker bus, towering above but held fast by the traffic milling about it. There wasn't a breath of air in the streets or in our hotel. A slowly-revolving fan set into the high ceiling of my room made a token attempt to stir up the humid atmosphere, but any effect it had was dissipated before it reached me.

I slept badly that night. I itched all over and no amount of cold showering could soothe the irritation. I could not bear my skin to come into contact with any sort of covering and, whenever I did slip into a fitful doze, I would awake soon afterwards, perspiring and more tired than when I had fallen asleep. Such nights were to be the norm from now on and, although most of us learnt to bear them, we all suffered from the heat. From the time we arrived in Lahore until we reached the foothills of the Himalayas, and again on our return journey from the Nepalese border to the Khyber Pass, the heat became our chief preoccupation.

CHAPTER 7

India

Unless one is totally without a conscience one cannot contemplate visiting India without considering one's attitude to the poverty which is certain to be encountered. Pakistan is hardly a rich country, but India is worse. Whereas in Lahore the motor-scooter trishaw had been the lowest form of taxi, in Ferozepore, the first Indian town we came to, it was the pedal trishaw. There were dozens of them, none of their riders looking much over thirty, which was hardly surprising for the strain on heart and muscles is terrific and can only be endured by young and relatively fit men.

We stayed in Ferozepore in a Christian school; we had been invited there by the headmaster, whom Roger chanced to meet in the bazaar. When he heard that the dak bungalow was occupied by officials, the headmaster insisted we stay with him. He had pressed us all to supper, but this would have been too much of an imposition and we prepared our own, returning later in the evening to the school to join some of the teachers for coffee.

For the first time for many weeks we found ourselves in a society where women mixed freely with men, a number of the teachers sitting with us in the headmaster's room being girls just out of training college. The school was sparsely furnished, without desks or exercise books, the pupils sitting on the floor and writing on slates, but the headmaster said that in twenty years he had seen his country slowly grow more prosperous. 'Some farmers,' he said, 'have too much money; they only spend it on evenings in town and buying tractors.' He told us that his son was studying in the USA; he feared that he might wish to stay on there after his university education was complete, which would be sad, for although he understood the attractions of Western society, India needed graduates and trained technicians for its schools and colleges and industries.

Next morning we rejoined the Grand Trunk Road and found ourselves in a landscape which day after day hardly varied. It was flat and mostly brown, although sometimes we would pass through more verdant areas of paddy fields, and there were always trees to add a further touch of green. Like Kipling's Kim we found that the chief attraction of journeying along the Grand Trunk Road was the travellers upon it.

The elephants and camel trains may not be as familiar a sight as they were in Kipling's time, although they have not entirely gone. Bullocks and donkeys abound, whilst chipmunks dart across the tarmac, parakeets flit about the lower branches of the trees and bald-headed vultures lurk hunched up on the highest ones. One may still see holy men. Motor traffic is relatively light outside the larger towns and cities, consisting mostly of grey painted Mercedes lorries, manufactured under licence in India. There are a few buses and some private cars, but for much the largest section of the population the train remains the normal form of long-distance transport. The Grand Trunk Road parallels the railway for much of its length.

The road is wide and straight, but this is not such an ideal state of affairs as it might sound for only the centre section, just wide enough for two motors to stand side by side, is metalled; in practice, when two vehicles approach, each has to pull to the left with the consequence that their nearside wheels drop into the far from soft verge. The course favoured by the bolder of the drivers is to proceed at such a pace that the vehicle skims across the ruts, but this demands not only a fair amount of skill and nerve but also a certain lack of concern for less agile road users, of which there are many. We settled for a somewhat erratic progress across India, zigzagging back and forth, decelerating and speeding up again as we dipped in and out of the rough. We soon discovered that if we pulled to the left too soon our opponent took this as an admission of defeat and triumphantly held to his course down the middle, with the result that we would end up with all four wheels on the verge and our passengers in the back nearly bounced out of their seats. We therefore soon learned to adopt retaliatory tactics, which consisted of edging over to the right, instead of to the left, whenever an approaching vehicle hove into sight. This usually so nonplussed the driver that he was only too pleased to make way for us; if he didn't, we had plenty of time to get back on to our own side, or even to quit the road altogether. During such manoeuvres, the passengers in the back of the lorry had a nerve-racking time when they suddenly found themselves proceeding in an unanticipated direction.

Almost as upsetting to those of a nervous disposition were our encounters with bullock carts. One would have supposed that, with their solid, unsprung, wooden wheels, all surfaces registered as equally unsympathetic, but apparently not, for their drivers insisted on holding the middle of the road until a motor vehicle was almost upon them and only at the last minute would they take to the verge. Actually it was the bullocks which as often as not made the decision to shift, for the driver might very likely be stretched out the length of his narrow cart, fast asleep; one could hardly blame him for at the rate his motive power covered the long straight road it must have seemed endless.

It may be that someone has counted all the bicycles in India, but if so he must have been a very old man when he ticked off the last one. Most commonly seen in towns and cities, cyclists are also a feature of every highway and, although most of those we encountered handled their machines with perfect confidence, there were a few who would have been better advised not to have gone near one. They caused us some anxious moments, the closest we came to real disaster being when a young man came pedalling out of a side turning, quite oblivious of us, his eyes raised to heaven, his thoughts obviously on much loftier things than mere survival. He all but went under the lorry's wheels, suddenly became aware of our presence, pedalled madly to try to keep ahead of us, and finally swung to the right and fell off behind a tree.

A buffalo and camel team near Amritsar, India

The various impediments to high speed motoring on the Grand Trunk Road ensured that we achieved nothing very ambitious in the way of daily mileages and were happy enough to reach Delhi in the middle of the morning of our second full day in India. There are guide books which will tell you that top quality hotels and restaurants in New Delhi are as expensive as those in Europe and America. Our experience was that a comfortable, air-conditioned hotel in the centre of Delhi was very cheap, and that a superb fresh salmon salad of immense size and complexity, beautifully served in most luxurious surroundings came to a little over £1. The mere memory of such a meal kept one going for days afterwards. It may be thought that when presented with the opportunity of sampling the best Indian cuisine, we would have chosen a curry, but fond though most of us were of this dish, we had already consumed considerable quantities of it, in many guises. On one occasion, so Jim alleged, we were even offered curried ice cream, and we welcomed the chance of something different.

Anyone who visits Delhi in summer will be chiefly occupied in defying the attempts of the climate to turn him into a wisp of steam. In our short stay of three days we made a number of sorties on to the streets, only to be driven back each time into the refuge of an air-conditioned shop or restaurant and we consumed bucketfuls of iced coffee. Fortunately, our hotel was situated on Connaught Circus, the heart of New Delhi, and we were able to stagger as far as the cinema farther round the circus, where we sat through a performance of *The Sound of Music* and a trailer for an Indian film, both of which seemed to be conceived much on the same lines, in that the scenery was very nice and whenever the action threatened to become too permissive the principals and everyone else within camera range would burst into song.

We also paid a visit to a department store on the Janpath, a wide thoroughfare which sets out from Connaught Circus as though it were going to emulate Regent Street and then half-way along its two-mile length changes its mind and does a very fair imitation of Whitehall. Our chief purpose was to equip ourselves with something rather more suitable for the climate than our Afghan coats and leather boots. There is much to be said for wearing all-enveloping clothes in hot climate, though most of us settled for shorts and loose cotton shirts. Roger, however, bought a dhoti, which he so arranged that it resembled a long kilt.

One cannot concern oneself overmuch about appearances on an overland journey, although on one trip we had a girl who would emerge from her sleeping-bag wearing a different set of ear-rings each morning and however rough the going looked as if she had just walked out of a hairdressers. The rest of us were content if we could get one good wash each day and put a comb through our hair, and if we hardly looked like fashion plates neither did we resemble too closely the more extreme proponents of the drop-out cult. Most of us tried to keep something respectable at the bottom of our cases on the off chance that we might suddenly be summoned into the ranks of society. On this shopping expedition, we were made to feel distinctly third rate by the assistants in the stores on the Janpath. Dignified and elegant in their saris, they stood aloof and motionless like goddesses from a Hindu temple. While Western dress is quite commonly worn by Indian businessmen, it is more unusual for women to forsake the sari; it is an ideal garment for the climate and bestows upon the wearer a poise hard to achieve in a dress or skirt. Indeed we saw a number of European women wearing it.

If obliged to move beyond the immediate vicinity of Connaught Circus, we resorted to taxis, an extravagance not often to be contemplated in other cities, but hardly one at all in Delhi. The city possesses an excellent bus service, but the big red double-deckers are designed to accommodate passengers in great numbers rather than in comfort. Delhi taxis come in three varieties, the most superior being family-sized saloons, usually Commodores, built in India and virtually identical in appearance to the Morris Oxford of the mid-1950s. Then there is a sort of motor-cycle combination, but with the sidecar placed behind instead of alongside the driver, so that it is really another version of the scooter trishaw, the cheapest kind of taxi.

Our sorties in one or other of these conveyances were chiefly concerned with matters of diplomacy, either to the Nepalese Embassy to arrange for visas, or to the British one to collect our mail and dispose of two of our passengers, Jack and Fred. They were a couple of lads from the East End of London and on their passports were described as car mechanics. It is true that they attempted to assist us at various times in tinkering with the lorries, but we later discovered that their chief connection with the motor trade had consisted of patrolling the streets of Whitechapel and Bethnal Green in the dead of night removing wheels from parked Ford Anglias. In the end their collection had grown to embarrassing proportions, quite outstripping demand, and they had decided to decamp with the proceeds. The result was their trip with us to India.

Jack and Fred were a humorous pair, though never before noon. Until then they would almost invariably be sleeping off the effects of the previous night's carousing; it was remarkable how often in countries where alcohol was not readily come by they managed to sniff out the local source. Their intention was to see how far around the world they could get in this manner before their funds gave out, and Delhi proved to be the limit. The British Embassy has a set routine for the many Jacks and Freds who pass through its hands; it provides them with a ticket home and a temporary passport for the trip, at the same time confiscating their proper one. They get it back when they have repaid their fare. The embassy staff were nothing if not courteous, but a certain coldness in their welcome to us could be detected. Whilst not a regular occurrence, there had been previous instances of poverty-struck overlanders requiring repatriation. Janet herself had once become so ill in Delhi that she too had had to be sent home, although she had been able to finance herself. We were further remembered on account of the 'Dent in the Embassy'. The entrance to the building was by way of a low arch, sufficient to allow cars to pass under it, but rather a tight fit for anything larger. Just how tight Roger had not appreciated until, on his previous visit, he had removed a piece of the masonry with the roof of his motor coach, the chip remaining as memorial to that particular overland expedition through India. The embassy is situated in part of the huge government complex, begun when the British moved the capital back to Delhi from Calcutta, but not finished before Independence and indeed hardly complete even yet. Sir Edwin Lutyens, the chief architect of New Delhi, was much addicted to the Renaissance style, an obsession he took to such lengths that even the Viceroy, Lord Hardinge, insisted on at least a grudging nod in the direction of native forms.

The most impressive example of Indian architecture in the old section of Delhi is the Red Fort—a huge fortress flanked by the railway and the Yamuna River—which takes its name from the colour of the sandstone used for the construction of its walls. Despite the fact that it was the stronghold of Moslem power in India, there seemed to be no shortage of Sikh guides waiting to escort visitors to view the white marbled Pearl Mosque, the site of the Peacock Throne and many more symbols of a dynasty and religion quite alien to Sikhism.

The Sikhs are perhaps the most easily identifiable of the many peoples of India on account of their turbans. These are worn because their religion does not permit them to cut their hair. For this reason, too, some of them tie up their beards in nets which they roll up under their chins. In the Punjab, that part of India and Pakistan extending from the North West Frontier to Delhi, Sikhs number some 15 per cent of the total population, Amritsar being the city in which they are most numerous. Until partition they had also been much in evidence in Lahore, but with the founding of Pakistan many fled eastwards, suffering in the process considerable casualties, and themselves wreaking much havoc amongst the Moslems, in the manner sadly familiar where differing religious communities exist within one nation.

In Agra, 120 miles south-east of Delhi, may be found 'the

most beautiful building in the world', at least in some people's estimation. Such a reputation is almost impossible to live up to and we were therefore prepared to allow the Taj Mahal a few blemishes. The story of its construction as a tomb for the wife of the Emperor Shahjahan, who was devoted to her and grief-stricken at her death in childbirth, has become almost as well known as the Taj Mahal itself and makes it difficult to judge simply on aesthetic merits.

The Taj is seen to its best advantage either by moonlight or early in the morning, from across the nearby River Jumna when the sun is still low in the eastern sky. As our stay was limited, we had to take it as we found it. We were staying some two miles away on the same side of the river. In other circumstances this might have constituted a pleasant evening walk, but in the heat of an Indian dusk such foolhardiness was out of the question. There appeared to be no motorised taxis about and Rachel and I were therefore compelled to take a pedal trishaw. Such a form of transport presents the passenger with an acute moral dilemma. Neither of us was particularly large, but then neither were any of the trishaw men. With each turn of the pedals they were shortening their lives, but on the other hand they were at least earning a living, and had they not been able to do so their lives would have been even shorter. As we lacked sufficient money to buy every pedal trishaw man in India a motorised vehicle, we therefore mounted up behind one and set off. For much of the way the road was level and we bowled along reasonably effortlessly, but towards the end of our journey we came to a slight rise and our speed dropped to a crawl as the driver strained away at the pedals. We feared to dismount and walk lest we offend the driver's dignity and we sat there trying to make ourselves as light as possible. It was a most uncomfortable experience, and we determined that we would pay off the driver for the return fare and walk, it now being dark and a little cooler, but he would have none of it and insisted that he wait whilst we viewed the Taj Mahal. We actually saw very little of it that night as the entrance was closed, but we were able to look through a chink in

Page 123 (*above*) The Sasaram–Arrah narrow-gauge train hauled by a Leeds-built steam engine, northern India; (*below*) various forms of transport in India, north of Patna, close to the Nepalese border

Page 124 (*above*) A waterpump in India in the grounds of a dak bungalow; (*below*) a mobile family planning unit which serves the Agra and Meerut area in India

the gate and catch a glimpse of a dome, cool, white and beautiful in the moonlight.

The following morning we drove the lorry up to the gate and parked outside. The view through the now open gateway was the familiar one of a dome mausoleum glistening beneath a cloudless blue sky. In front of it, the pool was filled with discarded cigarette packets, sweet papers and other litter. Yet, although we saw the Taj Mahal at a far from favourable time on an unpleasantly hot day, with the prospect of a tiring journey ahead of us and insufficient time to explore inside and around it, we could not fail to be aware of the special beauty of its proportions, of the intricate checkerboard pattern worked into the white marble and, above all, of the coolness within the great central dome.

The next 450 miles to Sasaram, where we turned northwards away from the Grand Trunk Road, became steadily more gruelling, the heat growing ever less bearable as we continued to head south. In addition, we were nearing the heart of the area of famine then raging in Bihar; each day we encountered more beggars, until at Varanasi (formerly Benares) we were hard put to make our way through them in the streets. Many had gone beyond the point of begging and lay inert on the ground, wrapped in loin cloths, waiting to die. Very likely some were already dead; it was impossible to tell, they were so still. Beggars were so common in India and, to a lesser extent, in Pakistan, that we soon came to accept them as part of the everyday scene, but in Varanasi their numbers and unusually pitiable plight forced us to take notice, although there was precious little we could do. Despite the famine, there was sufficient food in the kitchens of the station dining-room to provide us with a meal of bread and eggs.

As Varanasi figures on the agenda of virtually every tour of India, it may be hard to understand why few of us bothered to stir out of our hotel and explore during the only evening we were there. But every so often the overland traveller experiences a feeling of exhaustion, brought on by a combination of heat, an unfamiliar or inadequate diet and, chiefly, what seems to be never ceasing movement. At that point, there is nothing to be done but simply to do nothing. A good night's sleep nearly always restores the spirits; so it was with us. Perhaps if we had seen more of the city, if there had been no famine, if it had not been the hottest time of the year, with the smell and the dirt so all enveloping, our impressions of Varanasi might have been more favourable. As it was we were glad to leave a place where we had been chiefly aware of the heat and the dust, and much depressed by the sight of so many beggars.

Late in the afternoon after our departure, we turned away from the Grand Trunk Road and headed for Patna. From the junction at Sasaram for a good part of the way, the road ran along beside a narrow-gauge railway. Several times, although we were travelling at little more than 30mph, we quickly overhauled a train—a small, black, panting tank engine with a large chimney at its head, the grubby brown carriages festooned with passengers clinging to the hand-rails and foot-boards.

Patna is a good 150 miles south of Delhi, but the fact that we had to turn north to reach it induced in us the firm conviction that we had entered a more temperate climate and our spirits rose. In the city we found the best restaurant we had come across since leaving Delhi; there we consumed quantities of ice cream. With the knowledge that we were now not much more than a day's journey from the Himalayan foothills, the temperature hardly seemed to matter any more. We slept in a marquee erected in a park in the centre of the city. The next morning, a Sunday, we attended holy communion in a Victorian, brick-built church beside the Ganges. It would have looked vastly more at home in Dulwich than it did amongst the Moghul, Sikh and other fantasies of Patna, which included the former opium factory of the East India Company and what must be the most exotic granary in existence, the 90ft high Golghar, the brainchild of Warren Hastings and resembling, if it could be said to resemble anything at all, a giant beehive.

There were few worshippers inside the church; all were Indian, with the exception of the organist, an elderly Englishwoman, whose skin was lined and grey—evidence of a lifetime spent under Indian skies. We sang familiar hymns from *Ancient and Modern*, but we prayed for the president instead of the queen. All around the walls were memorials to Englishmen and women who had died and were buried in India, soldiers, administrators and businessmen and their wives and children. Nearest to our pew was one to an eighteen-year-old subaltern who had caught a fever soon after disembarking at Calcutta and had died before even reaching his regiment at Patna.

The road from Patna to the north is not a direct one, a detour being necessary in order to cross the Ganges. Janet and Roger suggested that some of us take the opportunity of sailing up the holy river; we could meet up with the lorry at the end of the day. So, whilst the main party continued by road, nine of us made our way down to the landing stage where we booked second-class tickets to Paleza Ghat. We boarded a paddle steamer, built by Dennys of Dumbarton just after World War II, and settled ourselves under the awning at the stern.

Passengers leaving a Ganges ferry boat, West Bihar, India

It is quite safe to claim that the Ganges is not like any other river, for there can be none so highly regarded by so many people. To the Hindu it is holy; therefore to bathe in it is a great religious experience, whilst to die beside it and have one's ashes scattered upon its waters is devoutly to be desired. On its 1,500-mile journey from the Himalayas to its many mouths south of Calcutta, the Ganges passes through the most densely populated regions of a densely populated country. Yet the waters possess remarkable properties, remaining pure despite continual pollution, in the form of sewage, decomposed corpses of men and animals, and debris of all kinds gathered up during times of flood. If anything we were reminded of the lower reaches of the Thames, with mud flats on either side, although the banks were somewhat closer and there were no distant hills and fewer signs of industry. We steamed for three hours down the wide, muddy waters, at one point passing a burning funeral pyre, which effectively dispelled any further comparisons with Canvey Island or Southend. We saw few vessels apart from the occasional black-sailed fishing boat and one ancient, stern-wheeled paddler. The breeze generated by the ship's motion and the steady splash of the paddles were in pleasant contrast to bouncing about in the back of the lorry and we dozed our way through the morning. At around noon the boat pulled across to the right bank, where we disembarked on to a rickety wooden landing stage, jutting out from a barren expanse of mud. A hundred yards off stood a line of railway carriages with a steam engine simmering at its head, the train and the rails being the only other evidence of human activity in sight.

Indian railways had become a familiar feature to us, but this was our first opportunity to travel on them. The appointments of our second-class compartment were decidedly on the primitive side; although there were four small fans fixed to the ceiling which did something, but not very much, to reduce the temperature, the ceiling was merely the white-painted underside of the wooden roof. The seats, arranged along the sides of the carriage, possessed neither backs nor upholstery, and it appeared as though there was no glass in the windows; for they had been lowered to their fullest extent, out of sight. I was suffering from a heavy cold and, having long ago run out of handkerchiefs, was reduced to continuous sniffing, which prompted a kindly gentleman in the corner of the carriage to proffer the advice that I ought to take some medicine.

Once on the move the heat became more tolerable and we sat

at the open doors, carefully avoiding the stains of betel-nut spittle on the floor. We rested our feet on the running boards and basked in the welcome draught as the train rumbled past brown fields and spiky palm trees at a steady 25mph.

A run of ten minutes brought us to Sonepore, a fairly large junction, and here we stopped for an hour. As is usual at Indian stations, entire families sat about surrounded by their worldly possessions. Despite the famine, a variety of foods was on sale, together with biliously vivid soft drinks displayed in huge round bottles. A small boy was peddling popcorn, the ingredients topped up by a layer of assorted insects, held fast by the toffee, and a dash of coal grit.

The grit is inseparable from the railway stations, where steam engines often reign supreme. The tracks are seldom fenced off and everyone is at liberty to wander across them or to use them in preference to the road. Sonepore Junction boasted a fair menagerie of animals, mostly mangy dogs, but some sleek-looking goats roamed the platforms and the tracks, foraging in and out of the wheels of stationary carriages and wagons.

I should not like to be a dog in India. The cow is holy; the elephant, of which we saw many north of Patna, is an aristocrat bestowing considerable status on his owner—the two may well spend all their working lives together; the camel, the bullock and the goat are useful and therefore cared for, but no one has time or food to spare for the dog. Consequently these sad, bedraggled creatures, possessing on average about two and a half sound legs apiece, seem mostly to be awaiting their end, either as a result of a well-aimed stone from a small boy or the wheel of a passing bus.

The hour's halt at the station passed pleasantly enough, as we watched the world go about its business. At the end of it, our black painted engine, bearing the initials of the North Eastern Railway in English on one side of its tender and in Hindi on the other, gave a mournful shriek and, emitting clouds of black smoke, set off once more. We stopped at each station along the line, giving small boys the opportunity to peddle food and drink and arrived at our destination, Muzziferpore, just in time for tea.

Roger and Janet had arrived in the lorry some time before, but we made them wait while he washed the coal dust from our hair and faces, and consumed tea and toast in the refreshment rooms.

We still had some miles to go that night if we were to keep to our schedule and reach the Nepalese border at lunchtime the following day. We drove through a landscape which, for the first time since crossing the Indus, offered some variety. Instead of brown fields, there was lush, swampy countryside, profusely planted with bushes and trees in full blossom, standing amongst pools of water. The weather, too, was transformed, and ahead of us a bank of black clouds loomed up, ominous against the red setting sun. Almost before the hood could be unrolled, a tremendous storm broke. Sheet after sheet of lightning illuminated the trees and the rain beat down with such force that it almost brought us to a standstill. It poured in through the seams and joins in the canvas canopy and ran down our necks. For half an hour we drove through the torrent, not daring to shelter under the trees for fear of the lightning.

As abruptly as it had begun, the storm ended, some flashes continuing for a little while longer in the dusk sky away to the south. We pulled off the road and turned into a long, overgrown drive. The branches on either side brushed against the lorry, spraying us with water, which turned to steam as it splashed on the warm earth. We drew up beside the wooden verandah of a dak bungalow. No light showed from inside, and with the lorry's engine switched off there was no sound save the rumble of distant thunder. For a moment we waited, undecided and apprehensive in the sudden stillness after the fury of the storm; then two or three of the passengers jumped down, climbed the creaking steps of the verandah and tried the front door. It swung open but revealed nothing. The only torch we possessed had by now given out and, with the aid of matches, we groped our way right around the verandah, pushing at doors; some of these gave way, others didn't, including one behind which Jim swore he could hear the sound of heavy breathing. At this the girls decided they would sleep outside on the verandah. No one had any inclination to explore the depths of the dark, silent house and we set up our beds either on the verandah or just inside the open door of one of the outside rooms. We lit the primus stoves, their flames revealing nothing beyond the faces of those bending over them, brewed some tea and then turned in for the night.

Waking the next morning I recollected having heard, faintly but distinctly on the hot, damp night air, just as I was falling asleep, the sound of a lone bugle playing the 'Last Post'. I half suspected I had dreamt it, but others said they had heard it too. No doubt it had emanated from some nearby barracks, but such was the atmosphere in the empty dak bungalow that had a squad of soldiers in red jackets and pith helmets come marching out of the gloom we should hardly have been surprised.

The sky was once again blue and cloudless. We arrived in Raxaul, the frontier town, at around eleven and carefully picked our way down the main street, past a couple of elephants and a great many pedal trishaws. The Nepalese customs and immigration officials were friendly and polite, but made sure that we had sufficient funds to finance our stay and to see us on our way again at the end of it. This precaution arose out of Nepal's experience with those young Europeans who come in search of a more satisfying creed and set of rules to live by than those they find in the West. Unfortunately few have the necessary stamina or dedication to pursue such a profound undertaking and tend to see the taking of drugs as a sort of magical short cut. As a result these young people become unproductive members of the community, an embarrassment not only to the Nepalese but to their own embassies, and their presence is not encouraged.

So much publicity has been focused on the international drug smuggling trail through Nepal and Afghanistan that one half expected to find a mob of emaciated addicts besieging the frontier post. In fact, such people make up only a very small proportion of Westerners visiting Nepal and one has to look hard to find them. That isn't to say we didn't come across pot smokers, even amongst our own passengers, but hashish is so widely smoked in Afghanistan and Nepal that this was hardly to be wondered at.

What is considered practical attire for an overland journey may appear to resemble that worn by hippies, but the true hippy is a rare bird and most travellers who are initially taken for such are merely pale imitations.

Our solvency established, the Nepalese bade us welcome to their country and at around three o'clock we set forth on the last eighty miles of our journey to Katmandu. The road was at first flat and well surfaced; had it so continued another couple of hours would have seen us at our destination. For twenty miles there was little variation in the altitude; then we entered the foothills of the Himalayas. Such was the transformation in the terrain that it was late the following afternoon before we passed through the city gateway and entered the Nepalese capital.

CHAPTER 8

Katmandu

The approach to Katmandu is superb. The road climbs the last summit and there below is the beautiful, fertile Katmandu Valley, with the city some half dozen miles away; beyond lie the Himalayas and, in front, the golden domes of Swayambhunath, the Monkey Temple, sparkling in the sunlight. As recently as twenty years ago, if one wanted to visit Katmandu one first had to obtain permission, which was denied to all but a very few. If one was among the favoured exceptions, one boarded a narrow-gauge train at the Indian frontier, stayed on it until the end of the line, which was no great way off, and then walked the last sixty miles. In 1953, a regular air service from India was started; the DC3 aircraft followed a somewhat hazardous route, swooping up the valleys and—usually—dodging the peaks. For some time, thereafter, any freight too bulky to fit inside a DC3's relatively small fuselage, or not urgently needed, continued to be carried over the mountains by a cable ropeway, as it had been for nearly fifty years. This ropeway was still in existence at the time of our visit, looping up and down the valleys and ridges, but had fallen into disuse since the opening of the road. It was this road which really brought the outside world to Nepal, transforming it in the process.

The official title of the road is the Tribhuvan Rajpath, after the late king, but it is more commonly known as the Rajpath. Built by Indian engineers, its completion was a tremendous achievement for its sixty-mile length encompasses quite enormous variations in altitude, beginning down on the plain at not much over 150ft above sea level and reaching 8,000ft at its highest point. Even more spectacular is the fact that, rather than achieving its summit at the end of a steady sixty-mile climb, it does so in something less than half this distance, having in the meantime passed over many lesser summits. It continues in this manner in a succession of dizzy descents and ascents until it reaches the 4,000–5,000ft high Katmandu plateau.

Unlike the mountains of northern Turkey and the Latterban and Khyber Passes, the foothills of the Himalayas presented a landscape of brilliant colour, chiefly the green of the trees and the stepped fields cut into the hillsides, with at various points the brown of bare rock, blood red blossom, and pale honeysuckle. For the first few miles, whenever the road twisted back on itself, we would catch a glimpse of the yellow plain of India stretching away to the south, shimmering in a heat haze, but it was soon hidden behind the hills, and we concentrated our gaze northwards. The day was sunny, with the temperature down to 70° F, a drop of some 25° since the previous morning, so that it felt almost cool. Concealed in the white clouds ahead of us were the highest mountains in the world and the question we were all asking was whether the clouds would part so that we might see them. From the experience of Janet and Roger, we knew they might remain hidden for days; also, if we were ever to see them, our best chance would be from the Rajpath, rather than from the lower altitude of Katmandu.

We continued for some miles, the bends and the gradient restricting us to little more than walking pace. Then, suddenly, to the north-west, higher in the sky than we had supposed even a Himalayan summit might be, there appeared, white amongst the white clouds but sharply defined by an outline of jagged rock, the 26,540ft peak of Annapurna. The sight was breathtaking, and we stopped the lorry and stared in wonder, until the clouds came together again and Annapurna faded back into the sky. We were most fortunate to be given such a dramatic introduction to the Himalayas. There were times during our stay in Katmandu when, under a cloudless sky, they filled the northern horizon; and, on our return down the Rajpath, we were able to make out Everest itself—which lies far to the north-east and consequently looks no higher than the nearer, lesser peaks—but nothing was quite so startling as that first brief revelation on the last day of our journey out from England.

Every few miles along the road, gangs of men were at work repairing the surface where it had crumbled away, or clearing rocks which had fallen from higher up. There was no retaining wall or fence and, at the narrowest places, one might find oneself steering within a matter of eighteen inches of a sheer drop of many hundreds of feet. So steep was the gradient, whether climbing or descending, that our speed hardly ever rose above 10mph and it wasn't until we were on the final plateau that Hope was able to move out of second gear. The regular drivers on the Rajpath, chiefly Sikhs, in charge of lorries and buses, manage to maintain a higher average rate of progress, but only at some risk. While we were in Katmandu there were rumours that one of the vehicles had gone over the edge, and a haulage firm plying the route took space in the local paper to announce that none of their lorries had been involved and business was continuing as usual.

Katmandu is the capital of Nepal for the very simple reason that it occupies the only large area of flat terrain north of the Terai, the mainly jungle lowland area in the south bordering on to India. Some half a million people, out of a total population of about 11 million, live in the Katmandu Valley. Not all of them are Nepalese; apart from members of the diplomatic corps and the inevitable Americans—who work in the hospital they have set up just outside the city and in the Peace Corps—there are also thousands of Tibetans. These are some of the lucky few who escaped when their country was invaded by the Chinese, a fate which some fifteen years ago appeared likely to overtake Nepal. Now, with India and China on much better terms, and China on better terms with practically everybody, the threat from the north has receded, although in Katmandu one is very aware of the proximity of China. It is actually nearer than India and easily accessible by a road newly built by the Chinese. Various goods manufactured in China are on sale in the shops of Katmandu, and one sees Chinese lorries in the streets. Initially, one takes these for Russian-built vehicles, which in turn look very like American ones of the World War II period, until one sees the Chinese markings on the bonnets. The Chinese themselves are less conspicuous, unlike the Americans; although the USA may be less directly involved in Nepal than in many Asian countries, Katmandu is figuring more prominently each year in the itineraries of American travel agencies and there are probably more US citizens in Nepal at any one time than any other foreigners, apart from Tibetans and Indians.

Rather in the manner of the Afghanis and their relationship with Russia and America, the Nepalese play off India against China. Their affections tend to lie with the former and they do not care for the official Chinese attitude towards the Buddhist faith, of which the fate of the Tibetans is a constant reminder. Nepal has always been closely linked economically with India and, until the coming of regular air services to Dacca and Bangkok, practically every visitor to the country had to pass through India. Intent on establishing its independence, this is somewhat irksome to Nepal and from time to time India has received broad hints from its small neighbour not to become too possessive.

Not only was Nepal, until twenty years ago, virtually forbidden territory to foreigners, it was equally difficult for the Nepalese to venture beyond their own frontiers. One who did was Jang Bahadur, ruler of the country in the latter part of the nineteenth century. He made a tour of Europe and met Queen Victoria. During his trip he was smitten with a passion for the classical style of architecture, evidence of which may be seen today in the large public buildings dotted amongst Katmandu's 2,000 pagodas. Instead of appearing incongruously out of place, they add to the charm of the city and to its already considerable fascination for the student of architecture. Equally remarkable are the carvings which are found everywhere, even on the most neglected and insignificant structures; they are of a most delicate design, though sometimes portraying most indelicate goings on.

As might be expected, Nepalese art and customs bear the imprint of both India and China. In the far south of the country the people are chiefly Hindus, in the north Buddhists, and in the middle a mixture of each, although principally Hindu. Religion is not simply an important part of the life of every Nepalese, but his whole life; virtually every action he takes reflects a religious attitude. The temple where he worships is also his supermarket and his social centre. In Katmandu, if one wants a haircut or a shave one goes along to the barber squatting on the steps of the pagoda. More than once when out in the evenings we found ourselves suddenly caught up in the middle of a procession of dancing, chanting men, women and children, wearing masks, banging gongs, and blowing wind instruments, as they wended their way through the narrow streets towards a temple.

One afternoon, during a walk up into the hills around the city, we discovered a statue of a goddess, slightly larger than life-size, set in an open grotto half-way up a steep path. At first it seemed she had been desecrated, for she was daubed all over with red and yellow dye, her private parts were obscured by a mass of crushed blossoms, and small children were playing about on top of her. In fact the dye and the blossoms had a religious significance and the children were simply learning to treat these symbols with the easy familiarity and affection which all Nepalese soon acquire.

The chief Buddhist place of worship in the Katmandu Valley is the Monkey Temple, or Swayambhunath, spectacularly planted on top of a precipitous wooded hill just outside the capital. Monkeys are sacred in Nepal, but the ones living in the temple didn't seem to have been told this and had no sense of dignity or decorum whatsoever. Rachel, who approached every new acquaintance, human or animal, with the attitude that it should be regarded as friendly until proved otherwise, nearly lost a finger during our visit. One monkey, showing no interest at all in the piece of bread she was holding, ran off chattering and spitting with frustrated rage when the finger was withdrawn a split second before the animal's teeth could sink into it.

The small boys of Katmandu take great delight in tossing stones at the monkeys, which may account for their evil temper.

The monkeys swarm all over the gilded roofs of the various temples and will often accompany visitors descending the steep steps to the valley; they swing from branch to branch, screeching and generally threatening to make a nuisance of themselves until the intruders have left their exclusive domain.

At most times of the day some sort of religious observance is taking place at Swayambhunath and our visit was to the accompaniment of a series of muffled drum beats and groans coming from the bowels of the largest of the temples. There is no better place to view the whole of Katmandu and its surroundings than from the top of the Monkey Temple hill. There one may look across the Bagamati River and the rickety string-and-wood bridge which one has just crossed to reach the temple, past the roof-tops of the city and the foothills all around it, to the snow peaks of the Himalayas. Beyond them, for the best part of a thousand miles, stretch range after range of mountains, at no point lower than 9,000ft.

The inhabitants of Katmandu are as attractive as their city, both Nepalese and Tibetans seeming to spend most of their time smiling at one another and at foreign visitors. The children are the friendliest imaginable, ever anxious to help. One delightful character we met was an eight-year-old Gurkha boy who worked in a tea-house, clearing away and washing up from early in the morning until late at night.

One afternoon we took a picnic up into the hills around the perimeter of the Katmandu Valley and stopped beside a mountain stream. We had plenty of wood and matches, but a stiff breeze foiled all our attempts to get a fire going. We had been followed for much of the way by four small children, who had squatted on the opposite bank and were watching us, giggling. Eventually one of them came shyly forward and, without saying anything, produced within a few seconds a steady flame which he quickly fanned into a fierce blaze.

Life can be hard for children in Nepal, particularly for those living outside the Katmandu Valley. Medical facilities in the hill villages are not plentiful, but the position is improving; and

A school bus in Katmandu, Nepal

down in the lowland jungles malaria is rife, although again much has been done of late to control it. Nevertheless, a Nepalese child stands only a fifty-fifty chance of surviving infancy. There are a number of schools in Katmandu for the children of the wealthier Nepalese. The older girls are to be seen in groups in the streets on their way to classes, dressed in western-style smocks and gym slips and carrying books, whilst the younger boys and girls travelled to school in small, ancient buses. There were two such buses, built in the late 1920s in the USA and imported in sections by way of the aerial ropeway; they were then put together and set to work in the valley, from which they had never departed. The side windows, bereft of glass, were fitted with canvas blinds in case the buses were caught in the rain, though one feared they might be battered quite to pieces in such an eventuality, so fragile was their appearance. They would bounce and sway along the not especially well surfaced city streets at regular intervals throughout the day, never exceeding 20mph, taking their cargoes of small Nepalis to school and back home again.

Despite the invasion of Katmandu by all manner of vehicles following the opening of the Rajpath, a number of the original ones brought in, like the buses, by the ropeway, survive, some of them entering their fifth decade. Several times we saw a beautifully maintained, chauffeur-driven American limousine, either conveying an elegant Nepalese lady or parked outside one of the larger shops. The only external indication of the effect of the passing of a good forty years being the yellowing of the safety glass and a whiff of blue smoke from the exhaust. There were also some ancient lorries at work; these were rather less than immaculate, none of them possessing much exterior paint and sporting tyres with patches not merely stuck on but in some cases neatly bolted.

A good deal of merchandise was moved around the city by way of one-manpower carts; much of the remainder was carried by donkeys, very little going by horse or motor. Horses were not common, the greatest number we saw together at any one time

Page 141 On the lower slopes of the Rajpath, Nepal

Page 142 (*left*) The Nepalese tea-house boy

(*right*) a leper begging near Katmandu

being when a female member of the royal family passed us by in the course of a shopping expedition. She sat in an open horse-drawn carriage with a large parasol held over her; although accompanied by various dignitaries and military gentlemen, her presence provoked no reaction whatsoever in the citizens. This suggested that such sights were commonplace or that royalty was not at that particular moment held in very high esteem.

There were a number of Western-style hotels and restaurants in Katmandu, some of which were surprisingly expensive. Among the few really cheap ones was the Camp, run by an Indian named Ravi, who provided simple meals, the most popular seeming to be jam pancakes. The only trouble with the Camp was that it was so well patronised by the younger and more impecunious of the Western tourists that one had often to wait a good half hour to be served. In the evenings, anyone who cared to could put on an entertainment at the Camp. Heather and Jill, the two sisters in our party, were quite accomplished folk singers, and performed there one night. Although they had a full house, it has to be confessed that not all our group attended, some of us having become almost as familiar as they were with their repertoire during the last two months.

We alternated between European and Tibetan establishments for our main meal of the day. Tibetan food, rather similar to Chinese, left one feeling hungry half an hour after a meal. The restaurants provided not only food but what were claimed to be genuine relics brought from monasteries in Tibet at the time of the Chinese invasion. These scrolls and carvings, all very beautiful, were pressed upon us at what we were assured were most reasonable prices. Experienced travellers had warned us that any such 'relic' offered for sale would almost certainly have been manufactured in one of the workshops set up in Katmandu to cash in on the booming tourist trade; whilst this may well have been true, they were at least produced by genuine Tibetans and most attractive, if beyond our pockets.

The time in Katmandu passed happily enough, sightseeing, sitting in the sun, talking and walking. Many people expressed interest in our beautiful lorry, but no one was able to bring himself to make a definite offer for it. One morning, at the request of a possible client, we drove out to the airport to see what could be done to repair a coach which had formerly belonged to Janet and had been used to ferry passengers from the airport to the city centre. It turned out that its chief need was new parts, which were unobtainable in Katmandu. Making the most of our excursion, we stayed to watch a DC3 take off for an airstrip in the mountains and a Pakistan International Friendship depart for Karachi. We also inspected, from a distance, sundry aircraft belonging to the king. An Indian pilot told us he had been flying into Katmandu for years, knew everything there was to know about the political situation there and assured us that the Chinese were about to invade.

We stayed on in the city for another five days, waiting to see if one of the various shadowy personages hovering around Hope would come up with a firm offer; then we decided that it was time to make a move. If we had got rid of Hope in Katmandu, it would have had to be for a sum sufficient to cover the costs of our journey back to Kabul. As we knew that Abbas was sure to find buyers for the lorries in Kabul eventually, there seemed little point in hanging about any longer. Beautiful though Katmandu was, none of us felt we could spend many more days inspecting its pagodas, walking its streets or indulging in its other now familiar delights, without boredom setting in. That would have been a sad end to it all, so we determined to leave.

CHAPTER 9

The Homeward Journey

The highlights and lowlights of our journey back to Kabul, and, indeed, from there on to England, seemed to revolve around encounters with public transport, not all of them intended and some we should have been happy to have done without. Our lorry's descent of the Rajpath, notable apart from the spectacular scenery for the only recorded case of Janet suffering from travel sickness, ended with the discovery that we had left a number of documents in our hotel in Katmandu. Jim was delegated to go back on the local bus to fetch them. He didn't much care for the prospect—only recently a party of twenty-five Indian pilgrims died when a bus went over the edge on its way down from Katmandu. But he went, rejoining us three days later at Patna after a series of adventures including a night in an Indian Railways sleeping berth, which he described as 'very like a luggage rack only less comfortable'.

Our band of original members was slowly diminishing, many having left us at Katmandu—Andy and Martin to go farther into the Himalayas, most of the others returning south to Calcutta and thence by sea or air to Australia. Tom was down to his last £5, but not for him an ignominious return without a passport using British Embassy funds. He cabled his landlady in Coventry and, rather to our surprise, back came a first-class air ticket home. Tom had other plans, however, and he exchanged it for one for Australia.

At Patna we said goodbye to Rachel and the two sisters, Heather and Jill. They too, were heading for Australia, although Jill's stay was a short one; within six months she was to return to England where she and Roger were married. Now our party was reduced to six—Janet, Roger, Jim, myself, Geoff, the last of our original passengers who was coming back as far as Lahore, and John, who joined us in Katmandu. The son of a British soldier who had been murdered in Israel by the Stern Gang in 1947, John had since lived with his mother in Australia and was returning to England for the first time.

We retraced our route from Patna along the narrow road beside the railway line and were some three-quarters of the way down it when, as was bound to happen sooner or later, we came up against a lorry travelling in the opposite direction which simply refused to budge from the centre of the road. Roger was driving at the time, he swung the wheel to the left, towards the railway, and almost immediately there were two loud reports and we bumped to a halt. Both nearside tyres were ripped to pieces by six-inch metal spikes which had been inexplicably planted between the road and the rails by the railway company. We carried one spare tyre and one jack, which left us with the problem of how to raise Hope on to an even keel; after that we should have to consider how, when, or where the tubes and tyres might be repaired or replaced. We sat down at the roadside under the meagre shade of an apology for a tree and cursed the Indian railways, the Indian lorry drivers, and ourselves for quitting England and embarking on such a silly venture. After a while we felt a bit better and foraged about for something to pack under the axles. Jim found some lumps of wood down a track and I discovered a few bricks in the corner of a cornfield; with these we set to work. By jacking up one end at a time, squeezing in a brick or a piece of wood, and then repeating the process at the other end, we slowly restored Hope's equilibrium. We were then able to remove the two diseased wheels and replace them by the one sound one. Unfortunately Hope had not been designed to operate as a three-wheeler, so we now had to set about obtaining replacement tyres. We had passed a sizeable town some five miles back and planned to wave down the next vehicle heading in that direction and ask for assistance. Had it been a motor-cycle combination or a man on a camel, we should have had to rethink our tactics, but for the first time that afternoon fortune decided to give us a break and an old Morris Commercial truck obligingly took Roger, myself and the two wheels aboard.

In the town we found a tyre store, whose owner smiled incredulously when we asked if he had any new tyres. Such luxuries were unobtainable, but he assured us that the gaping holes in the ones we had could be easily repaired. We should have to wait, as he had other clients to deal with first. Roger and I whiled away the hot afternoon drinking quantities of tea out of small glasses and chatting with anyone who would speak English.

One man asked if we had seen the Taj Mahal and we said we had and had he, and he replied that he hadn't; we asked why not and he smiled and said that it was a long way from his home and he could not afford the fare. We should be passing Agra in a couple of days and to us that seemed like hardly any time or distance at all, but then we had grown so used to a life of travelling that 500 miles meant very little. Certainly our method of travel was comparatively cheap, but to the average Indian, we must have appeared rich almost beyond comprehension.

By late afternoon our tyres were ready, roughly patched and hardly up to Department of Environment standards, but sufficient to get us back, with luck, to Kabul. We then had to find a conveyance. We had watched two trains pass by and briefly toyed with the idea of boarding one and, when we reached the lorry, rolling off the wheels whilst we jumped. The maximum speed of the trains was around 20mph, which permitted many of the passengers to hang outside the carriages rather than sit within, but we should probably have bowled over Janet or Jim and therefore decided against it. There was little motor activity on the road, but much pedalling of trishaws, as well as a procession of three richly decorated elephants and a camel. As it was now dark and we were getting desperate, we threw our scruples to the wind and asked a trishaw man if he would convey our tyres whilst we rode in a second vehicle. He gamely agreed and we manhandled the heavy wheels up behind him, but after a few hundred yards he found the going too heavy, so we paid him off and sat down beside the road once again and cogitated. An elephant would have been just the job, but the three we had seen had better things to do, being on their way to a wedding. Eventually, well into the evening, a lorry came by and we thankfully hauled ourselves and our tyres aboard and by nine o'clock Hope was roadworthy again.

It was now high summer and the heat grew ever more intense. We carried our water in *chattis*, earthenware pots which were very cheap and fragile; they were liable to disintegrate at the slightest knock, drenching whoever was carrying them, a pleasant sensation which lasted but a few minutes, leaving one with the problem of buying another *chatti* and finding water to put into it. One night the heat rendered sleep so elusive that I took sleeping tablets, which worked much too well for I stayed asleep for most of the next day and was quite unable to drive for a good twenty-four hours.

At Allahabad we came across a side of the Indian character we had not previously encountered. As we drove round a corner on the outskirts of the city, a large crowd, milling about in the middle of the road, blocked our way. We stopped, but could see no cause for the disturbance and very slowly began to edge our way through. At this some of the crowd waved in a far from friendly manner and one man, right in front of Hope, picked up a large stone and drew back his arm as though about to hurl the stone through the windscreen. I was sitting in the cab on the passenger side and involuntarily ducked, but Roger next to me leapt down into the middle of the crowd and remonstrated with the man, who looked astonished and put down his stone. Another came up and asked, in English, what was going on. Roger said that all he wanted to do was to be allowed to pass. The second man spoke to the first in Hindi and then said to Roger, 'Is he right?' which failed to shed a great deal of light on the situation. Roger climbed back aboard and drove slowly away, leaving the crowd arguing and us wondering what it had all been about.

In Britain photographers are accustomed to pointing their cameras at whatever tasks their fancy, clicking the shutter, and inspecting the result when the film is developed. Anyone venturing into foreign parts under the illusion that a similar system obtains there is due, sooner or later, for a rude awakening. Considering that I had received my warning and escaped scott free in Iran, what occurred at Ambala Cantt on our last evening in India was really nobody's fault but my own. We had stopped at the station for tea and afterwards, seeing a photogenic array of steam engines, which were producing clouds of black smoke and depositing grit on everything, including our curry, I wandered across the tracks and started taking pictures. Almost immediately I was summoned to the foreman's office and asked what I thought I was doing. I explained that I was merely a tourist attempting to take photographs but this was not accepted and the railway police were summoned. A sergeant conducted me across the lines to the police station. In the corner of the room was a cell; gripping the bars, were a gaunt pair of hands, the interior being too dark for me to make out their owner. The sergeant said he would have to call his chief; after a quarter of an hour he arrived, accompanied by no less a dignitary than the district magistrate attired in full ceremonial dress complete with plumed hat. It may have been that he had been called away from some official duty, but if his uniform was solely for my benefit then I began to think that I could consider myself lucky if I too did not end up in the cell. Roger and Janet were called in and the magistrate said that we should have known Ambala was a junction of great strategic importance and had been the target of Pakistani bombers during the fighting and how was he to know I wasn't a spy?

In the end we managed to convince the magistrate and the police chief that I was merely a misguided tourist, but to be on the safe side they confiscated my roll of film. As a postscript, I might mention that the following morning, at Ludihana station, I sought out the chief of the railway police and asked if I might take a picture of an engine standing opposite and he said, 'There is no need to ask, why don't you walk along the line to the shed, there are many engines there.'

In Peshawar, believing that lightning never strikes twice in the same place, we paid a second visit to the station dining-rooms and this time got a very adequate meal. At the end of it our old friend the waiter produced a sheaf of grubby pieces of paper, which turned out to be testimonials from satisfied customers, and we were invited to add our own comments. Resisting the temptation to itemise blow by blow our experience of a month earlier, we made a slightly tongue-in-cheek reference to the remarkable cuisine and service of the establishment. Judging by its reception, this was exactly what was required.

Although it was still distinctly hot as we reached the gateway guarding the Khyber Pass, the temperature as we headed north-west was steadily declining, and we anticipated the temperate climate of Kabul with some relish. It was then that I made a very unpleasant discovery. One is always warned, when travelling in these parts, not to leave anything lying around as it will certainly be removed. We always arranged that, when stopping for any length of time, someone should stay with the lorry, but as our numbers declined there were fewer people available to sit on guard. For the past few days, we had merely taken out our most valued possessions, tied the canvas flap firmly down, and tried to partake of our refreshment within sight of Hope. As far as the Khyber, not a bootlace had been missed. Then, while searching amongst the pile of luggage, I discovered that my case was gone. I had not had cause to use it for a couple of days as I had been living out of a haversack. The last occasion when any of us could positively recall seeing the case was at a dak bungalow between Lahore and Rawalpindi. I had little option but to make my way back there, on the off chance of finding it. The case contained all my exposed film of the trip, as well as clothes and a camera, and it had therefore to be pursued. The Kabul–Peshawar bus was making its way down the Pass and I hailed it and climbed aboard. At Peshawar, I took the train to Rawalpindi. There I had a three-hour wait, and at a little before midnight I joined the night mail for Lahore and Karachi. The name of the town where we thought the dak bungalow and my case might be was Gujrat, some one hundred miles east of Rawalpindi, though none of us was certain. I stretched out on my seat and slept so soundly that I nearly missed my destination; I just had time to glimpse the station nameboard and gather my wits and remaining possessions before the train restarted. I stood on the platform and watched the red tail lamp of the last carriage disappear into the night, then turned and took stock of my surroundings.

They were not very distinct, a faint glow from an oil light hanging from the platform awning providing the only source of illumination under a starless sky. It was just possible to make out a wooden bench at the end of which sat an old man wrapped in a blanket. I joined him and he moved up and insisted on my sharing his covering, which was appreciated as the night was relatively cool. The old man dozed off but I found sleep impossible. An hour later, the eastern sky began to lighten and slowly revealed first the shining rails, then the silhouette of the station buildings and the trees behind it, and then a road. I carefully relinquished my half of the blanket, leaving the old man snoring peacefully, and set off towards the town. A *tonga* jingled past me, then a couple of cyclists. A herd of hump-shouldered cattle was driven out of a field, and by the time I reached a crossroads ten minutes later the village had come to life. I was now back on the Grand Trunk Road and, if this was where I had left my case, then there should have been a dak bungalow on the corner. But there was only a group of people, waiting for a bus. I joined them, and when it arrived did my best to explain to the conductor that I would get off when we reached a town which possessed a dak bungalow in a certain position. The bus charged along at a great rate, considerably in excess of anything we had dared attempt in the lorry, never veering to left or right, regardless of other traffic, which at that time of day was thin. After a run of twenty miles we arrived at a town which looked rather familiar and possessed a dak bungalow on a corner.

I was pretty sure this was the one and alighted, although I felt the likelihood of my case having been left there was remote. I walked up the pathway to the door, found the proprietor, who was sweeping the hall, and asked him if he had seen a case. He thought for a few seconds and then shook his head. I was not greatly disappointed for it was the answer I had expected. I asked if I might look under the bed in which I had slept and he said I could, so I lifted up the cover and there, gathering dust, was my case. Nothing inside had been touched and I offered the proprietor a large tip, but nothing could persuade him to take it. Even now I wonder at my luck and shall for ever remain convinced of the remarkable honesty of Indians and Pakistanis.

My return journey back to Peshawar by train gave me the opportunity to talk to a number of Pakistanis. Whilst I was waiting on the platform to return to Rawalpindi I was approached by a ticket collector, wearing a severe expression and the usual immaculate uniform, who asked me if I realised that the American magazine I was reading was 'a very bad one'. I asked why and got the reply, 'It criticised our president last year, it should be banned.' I had a pretty good idea what was coming next and sat back whilst a well rehearsed diatribe against the USA and all things American flowed forth. As it ended, the train pulled in, hauled by a shiny new green diesel locomotive manufactured by ALCO of Schenectady, New York State, and bearing upon its nose the legend 'A gift from the USA'.

Pakistani carriages are considerably more decorative than Indian ones, being decked out in a livery of leaf green and cream with silver roofs and a plethora of gilt lettering. Internally the arrangements are similar to those in India, with unupholstered seats in the lower of the four classes and small windows fitted with shutters, which in this journey were most necessary as the passage of the train whipped up a choking yellow dust. The brief spring had given way to high summer and the landscape was browner than it had been even two days earlier. The train climbed through barren stony escarpments, a prelude to the foothills proper of the Himalayas, the Hindu Kush and the Pamirs far away on the northern horizon.

At Rawalpindi I lunched in style in the station dining-room, served by a butler—as a railway company waiter is called—dressed in the most magnificent of all the splendid uniforms in which the staff of Indian and Pakistani railways delighted. His long, white silk jacket was pulled in at the waist by a broad black leather belt and he wore a splendid gold turban with a white plume at the front held in place by a gold brooch. The appointments of the room were equally impressive. Elegant cane chairs were arranged around tables covered with sparkling white cloths, the cutlery was kept in a large mahogany dresser, and ticking away on the wall behind me was a sedate wooden-framed clock manufactured by Gillett & Johnston of Croydon in 1910.

I was engaged in conversation by another diner, an intelligent and erudite doctor, who had much of interest to tell me about Pakistan until he got on to the subject of his country's relations with India. I tried to steer him off the topic but he persisted and quoted 'official government statistics' to illustrate how Pakistan had been forced to go to war in defence of her honour, and boasted of the enormous number of casualties inflicted on the enemy and of the unparallelled heroism of his country's airmen and soldiers. It was, almost word for word, the reverse of what one had heard many times in India.

A large crowd had gathered on the platform to await the arrival of the Karachi–Peshawar express. A fair proportion apparently consisted of the Rawalpindi male voice choir; some thirty or so men of varying ages, dressed in white suits with garlands around their necks, stood there singing and chanting. Every few minutes they would take a stroll to the far end of the platform and back again, singing all the while; during one of these promenades three of the group broke away and came over to where I stood. They inquired politely who I was and what I was doing in Rawalpindi and translated my answers to others who had now joined us. They asked whether I was a holy man, a question probably prompted by my beard and St Christopher's medal rather than any particular air of sanctity I might have been affecting. The singing was to celebrate a special occasion, they told me; a friend was expected home from a pilgrimage to Mecca. As the train pulled in, the pilgrim appeared at a carriage doorway. He was a tiny little man of about seventy, with a benign expression exactly as one would expect a pilgrim to have. He was absolutely besieged, garland upon garland being placed around his neck until he completely disappeared, only to pop up shoulder high in the middle of the singing throng. They bore him away, over the footbridge and out of the station, the three men to whom I had been speaking breaking away to place garlands around my neck and to shake my hand. The garlands were very simple and attractive, made of daisies, buttercups and pieces of tinsel; I still have one, pressed between the pages of a book.

Although the Peshawar train was described in the timetable as an express, it didn't take this too seriously, refusing no reasonable request to stop, pausing at many wayside stations and, at one point, just before the Attock bridge, coming to a halt in the middle of nowhere. A good third of the passengers clambered down from their compartments and strolled about until the driver sounded a blast on his whistle, at which they all climbed aboard with the exception of an old man who was relieving himself. The crew had noted his predicament, however, and held the train until he was ready to rejoin it.

Sitting opposite me was a fierce looking character from the North West Frontier, with a swarthy, lined face and black, straggling beard, and dressed in a kaftan and turban. After eyeing me intently for some five minutes he whipped out from under the folds of his clothing a long curved knife. Before I could make up my mind whether or not to leap through the window, he produced with his other hand from another section of his attire a cucumber. This he carefully sliced into sections and then looked up, baring a row of broken, yellowed teeth, and offered me some. He told me he owned a barber's shop in Peshawar and would be delighted to give me a haircut anytime I cared to call.

My last, like the first, social contact with Pakistan was in the European-style dining-room at Peshawar station. I was greeted by our old friend the waiter, who said, 'Welcome, come in, please sit down.' He waited until I had arranged my luggage and was settled at my table and then announced, 'We are closed.'

Next morning I booked a seat on the little Afghan bus to Kabul and, by the middle of the afternoon, was back once more amongst the donkeys, the squads of shabbily dressed soldiers, the carpet sellers, and the camel trains of Jadi Maiwand. Kabul was by now something of a second home, but I discovered on entering the Khyber Restaurant and meeting up again with Roger, Jim and Janet that one familiar figure was missing. Abbas was said to be away on a business trip, but no one knew, or at any rate cared to say, where. He might have been in Herat or he might have been in Germany, and the unworthy suspicion crossed our minds that he might have disappeared because he had had no success in disposing of our two lorries.

His absence was something of a blow for it meant we should have to make our own contacts and conduct lengthy negotiations with various government officials who might not speak, or choose to speak, English. Roger had picked up a few words of Afghani and we managed, but it was all rather wearing. Strictly speaking, the import of vehicles into Afghanistan was restricted and tightly controlled, but in the East strictness is negotiable and, providing one can reach an amicable understanding with certain key officials, few goals are unattainable. At the end of a week, we had found prospective buyers for all three lorries and, although the price offered was less than we had hoped, it was by now a matter of cutting our losses as quickly as possible.

One of the formalities insisted upon was that a recognised mechanic be found who would guarantee to service any vehicle brought into the country. We therefore approached the Bedford agent, a Pakistani, who considered our proposition and then regretfully declined it. That seemed to be that, so I departed. Roger, however, stayed behind and a couple of minutes later joined me, £50 to the worse but with the guarantee agreed and signed. At one point the negotiations came to a deadlock and Roger had his passport confiscated. Perhaps it was merely an unusually devious move in the game; at any rate it required the authority of the British ambassador to get it back, and more largesse had to be spread before the business could be concluded.

Second home or not, we were by now prepared to make the fastest possible exit from Kabul and for the first time during our journeyings we took to the air. There is a twice-weekly flight from Kabul via Tashkent to Moscow, operated jointly by the Afghan Ariana Airlines and Aeroflot. It is possible to book right through to London by this route at little more than half the fare charged on the Ariana/BOAC service via Beirut. The flight via Tashkent had the added attraction that one was offered the choice of continuing on from Moscow either by air or by train. The previous winter we had taken advantage of this and stayed for two days in Moscow before returning by rail via Poland and Berlin to the Hook of Holland and thence by boat home. Organised by Intourist, the trip had been good value for money, our stay in Moscow including two nights in an excellent, if old-fashioned hotel on Red Square, an evening at the opera, a conducted tour of part of the Kremlin, homage at Lenin's tomb and a walk through a real Russian snowstorm.

On this occasion, not being sure when we would get away from Kabul, we had not been able to avail ourselves of Intourist's services and merely booked air tickets to Moscow. We took off from Kabul on a clear, sunny morning, circled to gain height over the city—a green oasis in a land of bare, yellow brown mountains—and headed north. Our aircraft, an Afghan DC6, had formerly been the property of Pan-American, who still seemed to have a stake in it in that it supplied the sugar, most of the passengers and the crew.

For the first quarter of an hour of the flight we were below the highest peaks, banking through gorges, climbing all the while until we rose beyond the snow line and at 25,000ft levelled out. Beneath us was the Oxus, the border between Afghanistan and Russia, and to the east somewhere high in the remotest, uninhabited regions of the Hindu Kush, lay the westernmost tip of China.

Tashkent, an ancient city, at the eastern edge of the great Turkestan Plain, could be seen from the air to have developed into a largely industrial one. The plane landed and taxied through lines of Aeroflot jets up to the terminal buildings. We were admitted into Russia under the stern gaze of a large, middle-aged woman in a white overall who inspected us and our inoculation certificates with cold, pale blue eyes. We transferred into an Ilyushin 18, a turbo-prop machine rather like a Vanguard, which flew us efficiently and uneventfully for six and a half hours above the clouds before descending through them to deposit us in Moscow on a hot Sunday evening.

Most Westerners arriving in the Russian capital have already booked their accommodation, and anyone who hasn't seems to throw the airport staff into a state of confusion. We found ourselves in a Catch 22 situation; while the airport had no facilities for changing money, and roubles were not supposed to be brought into the country, we had no way of paying for a taxi or bus to take us into the city. In fact, I had kept a couple of roubles as souvenirs from my previous visit. The receptionist said we would find accommodation at the Aeroflot Hotel and what a pity it was we had no money to get us there. He kept repeating this with such emphasis that eventually, although very aware of the strictness of Russian currency regulations, I opened my wallet and exclaimed, 'Goodness, I have some roubles.' At this there were sighs of relief all round and we were bundled into a Moskovitch saloon and sent packing.

The least expected aspect of life in Moscow, so far as we were concerned, was its informality and at times downright inefficiency. Before our first visit we had imagined that everything ran like clockwork, and although it sometimes did, just as often it didn't. The Intourist traveller was issued with a book of vouchers, for meals, tours, taxis and so on, which meant he hardly needed to handle money. It had sounded very convenient, but someone had unfortunately muddled our vouchers, with the consequence that we found ourselves entitled to two lunches each, but no breakfasts. It wouldn't have been so bad had it been the other way around, but, as it was, when we came down the first morning we had to queue up at the reception desk, along with some dozen other visitors all in the same predicament, and sort it all out with a harassed lady who obviously thought the whole thing was a dastardly capitalist plot. She took a great deal of persuading that we were after nothing more sinister than our breakfasts, which we eventually got just before lunchtime. Once matters had been straightened out, everything worked perfectly, the harassed lady was transformed, beaming at us whenever we passed her desk. She asked if we would be home in time for Christmas; the porters were obliging, providing they were well tipped, and the only hiccup in the system was a phone call to one of our rooms at three o'clock in the morning when a voice asked, in English, if we wanted a taxi at seven. Apparently all tourists are given the once-over by the security police, or so regular travellers to Russia allege, and such phone calls are to make sure one is safely tucked up in bed and not out somewhere one shouldn't be.

On that previous visit, in mid December, it had been as cold and with as much snow on the ground as everyone felt was right and proper for Moscow at that time of the year. Now, however, at the end of May it was so hot, despite a brief thunderstorm, that we might have been back in Delhi. Once again sleep became elusive and, by four in the morning, it was broad daylight. There being no point in remaining in bed, I got up and took a stroll towards the city centre. The early morning trams were already on the streets; many of their drivers were women, some middle aged and dour looking, but others in their early twenties and apparently full of the joys of spring. One even turned and waved to me as I pointed the camera at her antiquated vehicle. I quickly put it away when I found it was also pointed at a barracks across the road, guarded by a soldier with a rifle who glowered in my direction.

It took no time to discover that Russia was far from being a classless society; this was particularly apparent in the eating

Page 159 (*above*) The outskirts of Katmandu; (*below*) Hope and Roger and contrasting styles of architecture in Katmandu

Page 160 (*above*) The splendid early 1930s Ford limousine seen in Katmandu; (*below*) a typical street scene in Katmandu

places. We had breakfast in an adequate, if sparsely furnished, self-service café, reminiscent of a wartime British restaurant, its customers mainly manual and office workers. For lunch, we tried somewhere rather different. On the other side of the street was a far superior eating establishment, patronised by businessmen and women; it was furnished, like most Russian interiors with pretensions towards the high life, in the Edwardian style. The tables, chairs and panelling were of mahogany, heavy and ornate; the tablecloths, very white and edged with lace, reached almost to the floor; the silverware was as far removed from severe functionalism as the furniture, and the view through the windows was almost completely obscured by several thicknesses of net curtains. Although the food was good, it was served at a painfully slow pace and people seemed quite prepared to spend at least an hour and a half over their meal. The restaurant was part of a hotel and from another room nearby drifted the familiar sound of selections from the Lennon and McCartney song book. This came as less of a surprise than it might have done, as we had already discovered that quite a lot of Western music and a fair number of films got into Russia, or at any rate as far as the smart set in Moscow.

One of the greatest ideological surprises overtook us when we boarded our train, whose accommodation consisted of two classes—hard and soft. Journeys on Russian railways tend to be measured in days rather than hours; therefore most long-distance trains were made up of sleeping cars. In some of them the hard class could be very hard. The Helsinki train, which we boarded at twenty minutes to midnight at the Leningrad station, was an international express of considerable prestige, linking the principal cities of the USSR, yet we found that when we folded away the upper bunk in the morning we were expected to sit against an unupholstered seat back. No such spartan appointments confronted the soft-class passenger. Externally similar to the other carriages and all of them of very recent construction, internally the soft-class one exhibited an air of ornate capitalist splendour at its most decadent. The sides were painted a pinkish

A huge Russian steam engine in a yard in Moscow

shade of grey, edged with varnished mahogany; engraved glass lampshades hung from the embossed ceiling; the panelled mahogany doors were fitted with elaborate brass handles, while the pile on the carpets reached half-way up one's ankles—all of this being faintly visible in the small amount of daylight permitted to filter between heavy red velvet curtains. One would have expected such a conveyance to have housed a prince and a couple of grand duchesses at least, but in fact it was provided for the use of a soberly dressed trade delegation which alighted at Vainikkala, the first station inside Finland.

Our departure from Russia, under the scrutiny of armed guards perched atop a high wooden tower amid a pine forest through which the line ran, virtually marked the end of our journey. Finland seemed so very unforeign, despite the architecture and the language; the people looked and dressed as they had in London when we had left three months earlier. One could hardly say that of the Russians, who dressed rather more like the English of ten years earlier. In Helsinki, the hemlines of the skirts might be anywhere from the thigh to the ankle; trains were on time; buses were clean; there were no unmarked potholes in the pavements; no rubbish in the gutters; hot water flowed from the hot taps and cold from the cold; lavatories flushed when the chain was pulled; policemen occupied themselves with directing traffic and comforting lost children; and anyone who obviously had not some business to go about was so rare as to be an object of curiosity.

For months we had been able to live rather better than most of the inhabitants of the countries we had visited. Suddenly we had to do careful sums before deciding whether we could afford to buy a cup of coffee. A night in a hotel was out of the question but we managed to get accommodation in a youth hostel and met there a Japanese art student who presented us with a delicate and beautiful lithograph which he had printed. We encountered a number of Japanese during our short stay in Helsinki, many of them studying at the university, a result, our friend told us, of a quirk of history and a consequent bond between Finland and

Japan. This had been brought about by the latter's insistence after her defeat of Russia in 1902 that Finland be granted her independence.

The next afternoon we sailed for Stockholm. The steamer had only just resumed its regular run after the winter break and we had the saloon almost to ourselves. We were able to stretch out along the comfortable seats and slept soundly, awaking as we approached Stockholm at breakfast time the following day. Now we were anxious to be home and therefore saw little of the Swedish capital, preferring to take the train for Copenhagen. It was crowded and there was little sleep to be had that night in a compartment filled with eight people and all their luggage. At Halsingborg the train was shunted on to the ferry for the voyage across to Helsingor; thence it was a short journey beside the sea to Copenhagen and a transfer to the Holland–Scandinavian Express. We, and the train, took to sea again from Rodby Forge at the southernmost tip of Denmark to Puttgarden, where we entered Western Germany, the approach of the latter country being heralded by a group of large, elderly men sitting on the deck of the ferry alternately puffing at cigars and munching cold sausage.

A somewhat fearsomely complicated-looking, but very shiny, black steam engine, with red wheels, took us in charge at Hamburg and swiftly and efficiently swept us through fields of yellow mustard to the Dutch border where it made way for a small electric box. For the third night running we had to make do without a bed, this being the most uncomfortable of all, for the Hook of Holland–Harwich boat was so crowded that the best we could do was to find a sheltered space on the deck and attempt to snatch some rest wrapped up in our sleeping-bags. We had very little success and in the morning trooped wearily down the gangplank and on to Parkestone Quay. Whoever instigated the joke about British Rail food had obviously never breakfasted on the boat train from Harwich to Liverpool Street, for we had a wonderful meal which very nearly made up for all the economics we had been forced to exercise for the last three days.

Our journey ended on a fine, midsummer morning in London, three months, the best part of 20,000 miles, and an awful lot of lorry, bus, horse-propelled, train, ship and aeroplane rides away from the wet dark evening in Chatham when it had all begun.

Index